Predictive Modeling and the Ecology of Hunter-Gatherers of the Boreal Forest of Manitoba

David Ebert

BAR International Series 1221
2004

Published in 2016 by
BAR Publishing, Oxford

BAR International Series 1221

Predictive Modeling and the Ecology of Hunter-Gatherers of the Boreal Forest of Manitoba

ISBN 978 1 8417 1586 5

© D Ebert and the Publisher 2004

The author's moral rights under the 1988 UK Copyright,
Designs and Patents Act are hereby expressly asserted.

All rights reserved. No part of this work may be copied, reproduced, stored,
sold, distributed, scanned, saved in any form of digital format or transmitted
in any form digitally, without the written permission of the Publisher.

BAR Publishing is the trading name of British Archaeological Reports (Oxford) Ltd.
British Archaeological Reports was first incorporated in 1974 to publish the BAR
Series, International and British. In 1992 Hadrian Books Ltd became part of the BAR
group. This volume was originally published by Archaeopress in conjunction with
British Archaeological Reports (Oxford) Ltd / Hadrian Books Ltd, the Series principal
publisher, in 2004. This present volume is published by BAR Publishing, 2016.

Printed in England

BAR titles are available from:

        BAR Publishing
        122 Banbury Rd, Oxford, OX2 7BP, UK
EMAIL   info@barpublishing.com
PHONE +44 (0)1865 310431
  FAX   +44 (0)1865 316916
        www.barpublishing.com

Acknowledgements

Since this publication arose from my PhD dissertation research, there are many people to whom I owe a great deal of thanks. I would first like to thank my supervisor, Dr. Ariane Burke for her patience and her guidance. I also appreciate the contributions of my supervisory committee: Dr. Greg Monks, Dr. Scott Hamilton and Dr. Ken Kvamme. Each of these gentlemen have been extremely generous with their time and their advice. I know that this is a better thesis for their contributions and suggestions. Dr. R. Stedman and Dr. B. White have also served on my advisory committee as representatives for the Canadian Forestry Service, and I have appreciated their presence. Members of my examining committee I also owe a great debt. Dr. D. Barber and Dr. B. Kooyman stepped in to help form my committee and I appreciate their participation, especially since I know they have busy schedules.

A massive debt is owed to the Manitoba Model Forest and its partner organizations, which provided the data for this research and funding to conduct fieldwork. A special thank you to the directors of the Manitoba Model Forest Archaeological Predictive Modeling Project, Linda Larcombe and Virginia Petch, who recruited me for the project and employed me over several summers. The Steering Committee for the project has also been of great assistance in helping me look at predictive modeling from other viewpoints. Jennifer Lidgett deserves special kudos for bailing me out a few times when data or ArcView was being uncooperative. The students from Hollow Water, and my fellow crew supervisors, deserve a big hand for working in very difficult circumstances and for conducting a survey that had success beyond my wildest dreams.

Most of all I would like to thank the members of my family.

Dedicated to those who are no longer with us.

Table of Contents

Acknowledgements	i
Table of Contents	ii
List of Figures	iv
List of Tables	v
1.0 Introduction	1
1.1 Questions to be Addressed in this Research	1
1.2 Chapter Outline	1
2.0 Predictive Modeling	3
2.1 Inductive Modeling	3
2.2 Deductive Modeling	5
2.3 Methodological Considerations for Models	5
2.4 Extending the Application of Inductive Modeling	6
2.5 Cultural Land-Use Data and Predictive Modeling	6
2.5.1 Cultural Data in the Manitoba Model Forest (MbMF)	7
2.5.2 Cultural Versus Archaeological Significance	7
2.5.3 Temporal and Spatial Considerations with Cultural Data	7
2.6 Simulation	8
3.0 Optimal Foraging Theory	10
3.1 OFT Models	10
3.1.1 Diet Breadth Model	11
3.1.2 Patch Choice Model	12
3.1.4 Central Place Foraging	13
3.1.5 Anthropological Applications of Optimal Foraging Theory	14
3.2 Criticisms and Modifications of Optimal Foraging Theory	14
4.0 Hunter-Gatherers of the Boreal Forest	17
4.1 Boreal Forest Ethnography	17
4.1.1 Boreal Forest Social Organization	17
4.1.2 Socio-Territorial Organization	17
4.1.3 The Seasonal Round	18
4.1.4 Adaptations to the Boreal Forest	18
4.1.5 Acculturative Change and the Fur Trade	19
5.0 The Dataset	21
5.1 The Boreal Forest	21
5.1.1 The Manitoba Model Forest	22
5.2 Woodland Prehistory of the MbMF Region	24
5.2.1 The Laurel Phase	24
5.2.2 The Blackduck Phase	24
5.2.3 Western Woodland Algonkian Configuration	25
6.0 Methodology	26
6.1 Data Collection	26
6.2 Statistical Testing of the Variables	26
6.3 Preparation of Data for All Models	27
6.3.1 Environmental Variable Preparation	27
6.3.2 Economic Model Variable Preparation	28
6.4 The CARP Cultural/Environmental Model Construction	30
6.4.1 Methodology for Environmental Model	30
6.4.2 Methodology for Cultural Model	31
6.4.3 Methodology for the Combined Model	31
6.5 Logistic Regression Models	31
6.6 Evaluation of Models	33
6.6.1 Field Methods – Summer 2000	33
6.6.2 Field Methods – Summer 2001	36
7.0 Results	40
7.1 Cultural Environmental Model - CARP	40
7.2 Cultural Environmental Model – Logistic Regression	42
7.3 Economic Model – Logistic Regression	45
7.4 Cultural-Environmental-Economic Model – Logistic Regression	47

- 8.0 Discussion of Results ... 50
  - 8.1 Survey Statistic Evaluation ... 50
  - 8.2 Kolmogorov-Smirnov Testing ... 51
  - 8.3 Gain Statistic Evaluation ... 51
  - 8.4 Evaluation of Modeling Methods ... 51
  - 8.5 Evaluation of Predictor Variables ... 52
  - 8.6 Evaluation of Research Goals ... 54
    - 8.6.1 Modeling Methodology ... 54
    - 8.6.2 Predictor Variables ... 54
    - 8.6.3 Ecological Approaches to Modeling ... 54
- 9.0 Conclusion ... 55
  - 9.1 Implications for Heritage Resource Protection ... 55
  - 9.2 Evaluation of Predictive Modeling ... 55
  - 9.3 Evaluation of Predictor Variables ... 55
  - 9.4 Implications for the Discipline ... 55
  - 9.5 Implications of the Study for Other Groups ... 56
  - 9.6 Directions for Future Research ... 56
- References Cited ... 57
- Appendix 1: Site Database ... 65
- Appendix 2: Variable Statistical Testing ... 69
  - 1.0 Cultural Variables Statistical Testing ... 70
    - 1.1 Distance to Ceremonial Resources Statistical Testing ... 70
    - 1.2 Distance to Earth Resources Statistical Testing ... 70
    - 1.3 Distance to Faunal Resources Statistical Testing ... 71
    - 1.4 Distance to Industrial Resources Statistical Testing ... 71
    - 1.5 Distance to Local Resources Statistical Testing ... 72
    - 1.6 Distance to Trails and Cabins Statistical Testing ... 72
    - 1.7 Distance to Vegetative Resources Statistical Testing ... 73
  - 2.0 Economic Variable Statistical Testing ... 74
    - 2.1 Moose Habitat Suitability Index Statistical Testing ... 74
    - 2.2 Woodland Caribou Habitat Suitability Index Statistical Testing ... 74
  - 3.0 Environmental Variables Statistical Testing ... 75
    - 3.1 Aspect Statistical Testing ... 75
    - 3.2 Distance to Lakes Statistical Testing ... 75
    - 3.3 Distance to Rivers Statistical Testing ... 76
    - 3.4 Forest Resource Inventory Statistical Testing ... 76
    - 3.5 Slope Statistical Testing ... 77
- Appendix 3: Environmental Variable Weightings ... 79

List of Figures

Figure 1: Graphical Determination of Diet Breadth	12
Figure 2: Graphic Representation of MVT	13
Figure 3: Graphical determination of travel times	14
Figure 4: Boreal Forest Regions of Canada	22
Figure 5: Location of the Manitoba Model Forest	23
Figure 6: Location of the Study Area	23
Figure 7: Map Calculator and the addition of Slope Classes	29
Figure 8: Class Values in a Calculated Grid	30
Figure 9: Random Point Locations	32
Figure 10: The Summer 2000 Study Area	35
Figure 11: Location of the Rice River Survey Area	37
Figure 12: The Location of Beaver Creek	39
Figure 13: CARP Cultural-Environmental Model	41
Figure 14: Cultural Environmental Model by Logistic Regression	43
Figure 15: Economic Model by Logistic Regression	46
Figure 16: Cultural-Environmental-Economic Model by Logistic Regression	49

List of Tables

Table 1: Summary of the Goals, Domains of Choice, Benefits and Constraints of OFT	11
Table 2: Summary of Results for the CARP Cultural-Environmental Model	40
Table 3: Survey Statistic for CARP Cultural-Environmental Model	40
Table 4: Kolmogorov-Smirnov Test Results	40
Table 5: Gain Statistic for CARP	40
Table 6: Parameter Estimates for Variables	42
Table 7: Summary of Results for Cultural-Environmental Logistic Regression Model	42
Table 8: Survey Statistic for Cultural-Environmental Logistic Regression Model	44
Table 9: Kolmogorov-Smirnov Test of Significance Results	44
Table 10: Gain Statistic for Cultural-Environmental Logistic Regression Model	44
Table 11: Parameter Estimates for Economic Variables	44
Table 12: Summary of Self-Validation Results by SPSS	45
Table 13: Summary of Results of Economic Logistic Regression Model	46
Table 14: Survey Statistic for Economic Logistic Regression Model	46
Table 15: Kolmogorov-Smirnov Test of Significance Results	47
Table 16: Gain Statistic for Economic Logistic Regression Model	47
Table 17: Parameter Estimates for the Cultural-Environmental-Economic Model	48
Table 18: Model Self-Validation by SPSS	48
Table 19: Summary of Results for Cultural-Environmental-Economic Model	48
Table 20: Survey Statistic for Cultural-Environmental-Economic Logistic Regression Model	48
Table 21: Kolmogorov-Smirnov Test of Significance Results	48
Table 22: Gain Statistic for Cultural-Environmental-Economic Logistic Regression Model	48
Table 23: Survey Statistic Summary (% of Area:% of Sites)	50
Table 24: Summary of Kolmogorov-Smirnov Testing Results	50
Table 25: Gain Statistic Summary	50
Table 26: Borden Numbers of Woodland Sites in the Study Area	66
Table 27: Survey 2000 Site Discoveries	67
Table 28: Survey 2001 Site Discoveries	68
Table 29: Distance to Ceremonial Resources Statistical Testing	70
Table 30: Distance to Earth Resources Statistical Testing	70
Table 31: Distance to Faunal Resources Statistical Testing	71
Table 32: Distance to Industrial Resources Statistical Testing	71
Table 33: Distance to Local Resources Statistical Testing	72
Table 34: Distance to Local Resources Statistical Testing	72
Table 35: Distance to Vegetative Resources Statistical Testing	73
Table 36: Moose Habitat Suitability Index Statistical Testing	74
Table 37: Woodland Caribou Habitat Suitability Index Statistical Testing	74
Table 38: Aspect Statistical Testing	75
Table 39: Distance to Lakes Statistical Testing	75
Table 40: Distance to Rivers Statistical Testing	76
Table 41: Forest Resource Inventory Statistical Testing	76
Table 42: Slope Statistical Testing	77
Table 43: Aspect Class Weighting	80
Table 44: Distance to Lakes Class Weighting	80
Table 45: Distance to Rivers Class Weighting	80
Table 46: Forest Resource Inventory Weighting	80
Table 47: Slope Class Weighting	81

Chapter 1 - Introduction

1.0 Introduction

There are several reasons for archaeologists to develop and critically examine the use of archaeological predictive models (APM). APM has had an immense impact on the field of Cultural Resources Management (CRM) in North America. Natural resource extraction activities in North America, such as forestry operations and mining, impact large areas of land. Often these areas have had little archaeological work done in them and very little is known about the heritage resources that may be present. There is a very real danger that heritage resources will be heavily impacted by development. Predictive modeling can be used as a planning tool by forestry or mining companies and therefore provide a measure of protection to these resources.

European archaeologists have resisted the use of APM, despite its active development in North America. The reasons for this are likely twofold. First, archaeologists in the United Kingdom especially and in other regions of Europe reject APM on the basis that it is environmental determinism cloaked in scientific methodology. Second, archaeology in some European regions is heavily skewed to historic sites, and hunter-gatherer archaeology is not as widely practiced. APM is thought to be much more effective in predicting hunter-gatherer site locations, rather than the site locations of complex societies. It is hoped that by the development and critical assessment of APM that these concerns can be addressed and what is a potentially powerful archaeological tool can gain greater acceptance.

Another reason to examine APM can be found in the literature on predictive modeling. In reviewing the archaeological literature, it is apparent that modeling practices had become stuck in a proverbial "rut", with many of the same environmental variables reappearing in modeling studies time and time again. For the last twenty years, since the landmark publication of a volume of papers in early predictive modeling work (Judge and Sebastian, 1988), the literature has been filled with articles by archaeologists explaining their own approach to predictive modeling, but generally using similar techniques and variables. Modeling has become a process of repetition, rather than experimentation. While existing models seem to work and be able to predict archaeological site locations, new variable types are not being investigated. This research proposes significant new variables reviews their efficacy while also reviewing the relative worth of different types of model.

1.1 Questions to be Addressed in this Research

This research has resulted in the creation creates four models to predict site locations of boreal forest hunter-gatherers. Two of the models are created using cultural and environmental variables: one using the method first proposed by the Centre for Archaeological Resource Prediction (CARP) (Dalla Bona, 1994a, Dalla Bona, 1994b) and the other using logistic regression. The third model focuses on economic variables in creating a predictive model using logistic regression and the fourth is a model that combines economic, cultural and environmental variables to make predictions. The creation of several models allows for examination of several aspects of modeling, modeling methodology and model variables. The creation of two parallel cultural/environmental models (one using logistic regression and the other using the CARP method) allows a critical examination of these two methods of making archaeological predictions. Logistic regression is used more widely in the cultural resource management (CRM) industry but requires software outside of the GIS program to be employed to complete the work. The CARP-style model is a much simpler method but is not a true weighted value method, the problems with this method are addressed in section 8.6.

Second, the creation of models using different sets of predictor variables (*e.g.* cultural, economic or environmental) will provide a test of the relative merits of these predictive variables. Most predictive models rely on environmental variables; this research will examine other variables available for prediction, and assess how effective those variables are in predicting site location.

The economic model will provide an indirect test of optimal foraging theory, especially central place foraging. The assumption made when adopting economic variables is that economic decisions influence site location. If this is true, then site location in the target region employed in this research should be correlated with economic factors, such as the suitability of habitats for woodland caribou and moose.

Finally, this research tests the effectiveness of general ecological models of cultural behaviour as well as the relative merits of environmental/cultural and economic models. Furthermore, the research will test basic principles of cultural ecology at a time when many anthropologists are in the process of revising and updating this paradigm.

1.2 Chapter Outline

Chapter 2 introduces APM. The chapter discusses different approaches to predictive modeling and elements that must be considered in creating a model. Major criticisms of current predictive modeling practices are reviewed. Alternative data sources for predictive modeling are also discussed, particularly, traditional land-use information from First Nations communities. Problems and concerns with the use of these data are detailed in this chapter.

Chapter 3 focuses on optimal foraging theory. Optimal foraging theory provides a series of models that allows scientists studying the foraging behaviour of an organism to make predictions about what the organism should eat, where it should look for food, how long it should look for food in a single location and where to locate themselves in relation to resources. While this method was developed in biology, ultimately stemming from microeconomic theory, it has been applied to human foragers by anthropologists and archaeologists. A brief review of some of these applications is conducted. The premises of optimal foraging have been criticized, however, and these criticisms are reviewed.

The APM created in this research are used to predict site locations for boreal forest hunter-gatherers. Hunter-gatherers of the boreal forest are discussed in Chapter 4. General theory on the nature of hunter-gatherer spatial and social organization is briefly reviewed, before a more detailed review of the spatial and social organization of boreal forest hunter-gatherers. The role of acculturative change in traditional communities and the effect that it might have on our knowledge of boreal forest pre-contact peoples is also reviewed.

Chapter 5 introduces the archaeological dataset employed in this research, including: physiographic setting, the time periods of interest and the archaeological sites under investigation. The boreal forest is the physiographic setting of the study area, and it is described in the chapter. The APM are restricted to the late pre-contact period, for reasons discussed in Chapter 5. The culture-history of that period is also discussed in chapter 5.

Laboratory and field methodologies used for this research are detailed in Chapter 6. Laboratory methods include information on data collection and preparation. The computation methods used to create the models are detailed in this chapter, as are the methods used to evaluate the predictive power of the models created. The field methods section recounts the fieldwork undertaken in the summers of 2000 and 2001 to test and validate aspects of the models.

Chapter 7 presents the four APM models created. It also evaluates their predictive power, using both the pre-existing archaeological database (*i.e.* the modeling database), as well as the new sites discovered from the surveys of 2000 and 2001 through the use of the evaluation tools discussed in chapter 6.

Chapter 8 discusses the questions addressed by this research, and evaluates the APM models.

Chapter 9 offers suggestions as to the benefits of this research. It points out how this research contributes the advancement of method and theory in APM. The chapter discusses the usefulness of APM to forestry companies, with regards to the use of APM as a tool in the planning process of forestry management practices. Finally, the benefit to the community involved (Hollow Water) is examined.

Chapter 2 Archaeological Predictive Modeling

2.0 Predictive Modeling

Predictive modeling has become a tool of the cultural resource manager (Carmichael, 1990: 216). Most academic journals regularly contain articles reporting on predictive models and, sometimes vociferously, debating their merits. In archaeology, predictive models are designed to predict the location of sites or materials in a region, based either on a sample of the sites in the region or on theories of human behaviour (Kohler and Parker, 1986: 400). They are tools for projecting patterns or relationships between known archaeological resources and their settings into areas in which those patterns and relationships are unknown (Warren and Asch, 2000: 6). All predictive models are composed of three elements: 1) available knowledge or a body of information from which a model is derived (*i.e.* the archaeological database), 2) the method(s) used to transform this information into predictions (*i.e.* the predictive modeling methodology) and 3) the predictions themselves (*i.e.* the predictive model) (Warren, 1990a: 91-93).

In theory there are two types of APM. The most widely adopted nomenclature refers to the models as inductive or deductive (e.g. Kamermans and Wansleeben, 1999, Kohler, 1988). Various authors have proposed alternative nomenclatures, but for the sake of consistency, the terms inductive and deductive will be employed in this research. No matter what nomenclature is adopted, in practice the distinction between these two types of model is often not so clear (Kamermans and Wansleeben, 1999: 255). Researchers often borrow precepts from both types of model, producing hybrids of the two types. This hybridized approach offers the significant benefits of each of the approaches while minimizing the weaknesses. The strengths and weaknesses of inductive and deductive models are discussed below. It is truly inaccurate to refer to APMs as either inductive or deductive, as models are usually neither purely inductive nor deductive in nature.

2.1 Inductive Modeling

Inductive models make use of existing knowledge to forecast trends (Warren, 1990a: 91) and have been the most popular form of predictive modeling used in archaeology (Dalla Bona, 1994a). Inductive models have been variously named: intuitive, or associational (Altschul, 1988), empiric-correlative (Kohler and Parker, 1986) and correlative (Sebastian and Judge, 1988: 4, Marozas and Zack, 1990, Church et al., 2000). These models are probably best regarded as correlative. In general, inductive models seek correlations between known archaeological site locations and features of the modern environment. The approach is analogous to pattern recognition procedures in remote sensing image classification (Kvamme, 1992: 20). Most of the variables employed in inductive models recur, such as slope, aspect and distance to water (Kvamme, 1992: 25-27, Kvamme, 1985: 218-219, Kvamme and Jochim, 1989: 5-6). When choosing variables, archaeologists tend to prefer variables that are related to site locations, but not correlated to each other (Rose and Altschul, 1988: 185). This preference for non-correlated variables often poses practical problems. For example, slope and aspect are both derivatives of a digital elevation model (DEM), which describes the elevation of the environment, and therefore are correlated. Additionally, other DEM-derived variables are often employed in the inductive modeling process, such as topographic prominence, viewsheds and hillshade. So, while there is a stated preference for related, but uncorrelated, variables, this is seldom realized in practice.

The main assumption made in this type of modeling is that non-cultural aspects of environment are good predictors of site location (Marozas and Zack, 1990: 165). These non-cultural aspects of the environment tend to be components of the physical environment (Kamermans and Wansleeben, 1999: 225, Kohler, 1999: 37). Most often, modern environmental variables are used in the model as proxy variables. Therefore, one cannot say that a location was chosen because it was close to water or associated with certain types of vegetation, but rather that sites tend to co-occur with those modern features of the environment. Predictive modeling could be done with paleoenvironmental reconstructions for time period slices, but to date, this has not been done, as it increases the complexity of the modeling process and the amount of data required to create the model.

The tendency for archaeological sites to recur in particular environmental settings has been a staple of "archaeological gut instinct" for many years (Warren, 1990b: 201, Kuna and Adelsbergerova, 1995, Warren and Asch, 2000), so in a sense predictive modeling can be seen as a formalization of the "gut instinct". Inductive modeling takes an essentially cultural-ecological view of human settlement systems (Kohler, 1999: 32, Wheatley, 1993: 133). This means that there is a focus on the relationship between cultures and their environment and that environment is an important determinant of cultural behaviour. This has led some authors to criticize inductive modeling as "environmental determinism" (e.g. Gaffney and van Leusen, 1995).

The unit of analysis in inductive modeling is the land parcel, not the site (Warren, 1990a: 94). Focusing on the land parcel allows the GIS to use a raster data structure. In the ArcView environment the raster data structure is referred to as a "grid". Raster data environments offer many advantages, such as allowing the easy overlay of separate layers of data (Burrough, 1986: 36). In ArcView, it is necessary to use raster data layers, or "themes", in order to use map algebra procedures, which are crucial to the completion of a predictive model. Focusing on the land parcel also allows some framework for the predictions to be made, in that the parcel then holds the predictive value. Therefore, the selection of an appropriate land parcel unit size is an important step in the analysis. If a is parcel too large, then the landscape becomes too generalized. If a land parcel is too small, millions of calculations will have to be done to complete the model.

Two main approaches to construct an inductive model are identified in the literature: the intersection method and the weighted value method. The intersection method is the simpler of the two methods; it looks for areas where all of the desired environmental variables intersect (Dalla Bona, 1994a). The number of intersections becomes the determinant of the land parcel's predictive rank. This method is extremely simple and suggests that all factors are equally influential in the prediction of site locations. This may not always be the case, where some factors might have more weight in the prediction of site locations.

The weighted map layer approach has been the most popular, as it allows archaeologists to weight the predicting variables. It makes use of categorical or class-based map layers, wherein each variable is assigned a variable weight, which indicates its predictive strength (Brandt et al., 1992: 271, Dalla Bona, 1994a). One of the major weaknesses with this method is that by simply changing weights, exponentially different results may occur (Brandt et al., 1992: 271). Therefore, the process by which the weights are determined is crucial. One of the ways that weights can be determined is through the use of multivariate statistical procedures, such as logistic regression (Parker, 1985). Logistic regression is a procedure which considers the influence of several variables simultaneously on a response variable. In the case of APM, the response variable is site location. Kvamme (1990) proposes using one-sample statistical tests to examine the relationship between environmental variables and sites. In this method, the background environment is treated as a control, and statistically significant differences between the distribution of environmental features between sites and the background environment are sought (Kvamme, 1990). For continuous variables, such as slope, aspect or distance to water, the Kolmogorov Goodness-of-Fit test is used (Kvamme, 1990: 370). As with any significance test, two hypotheses are expressed. The null hypothesis (H_0) expresses a case where no relationship exists between response and test variables occurs. In other words, it expresses the negative option – that there is no statistical significance. The alternative hypothesis (H_a) expresses a case where there is a relationship. That is, it expresses the positive option – that there is a statistical significance. In the Kolmogorov-Smirnov test, the maximum difference between the cumulative percentage of distribution of sites and cells in the environment is compared with a critical value (Kvamme, 1990). If the maximum difference (D_{max}) exceeds the critical value (D), then the null hypothesis (H_0) must be rejected. If the null hypothesis is rejected then sites are considered to be not randomly distributed in the environment. The critical value for the Kolmogorov-Smirnov test is calculated by:

$$D = \frac{1.36}{\sqrt{n}}$$

where D is the critical value (at $\alpha = 0.05$) and n is the number of sites in the analysis. In cases where the maximum difference (D_{max}) does not exceed the critical value (D), then it is said that there is no significant statistical difference between distribution of sites in terms of a specific environmental variable and the occurrence of that variable in the wider environment. The 0.05 level of significance is chosen for this test, as it is the standard level used in APM. The advantage of employing GIS in this type of analysis is that the GIS is capable of handling the large number of calculations required to quantify the background environment in order to compute this test (Kvamme, 1990: 370).

Once a model is created, testing is paramount. This can be done solely through laboratory methods, such as red flag modeling (Altschul, 1990) or through statistical evaluation, such as a gain statistic (Kvamme, 1988a). In red flag modeling, sites with anomalous settings are examined for possible predictive variables that have been missed (Altschul, 1990). Red flag testing, therefore, is a process of re-iteration of the modeling process, exploring new variables which might explain why a site was predicted as being in a lower potential area, and trying to find ways to promote it to areas of higher potential. Models may also be tested using statistical evaluation methods, such as those presented in section 6.6.

Many practitioners have heavily criticized inductive modeling. Ebert (2000) provides the most unified and vociferous criticism of inductive modeling. Most commonly, predictive modeling, and archaeological computing more generally, is criticized as being a set of techniques in search of a body of theory (Ebert, 2000: 130, Church et al., 2000). Perhaps the most serious problem with current inductive modeling practices is the disregard of archaeological variables such as site function or site temporality, in order to create a comprehensive model. Presumably, sites with different functions in a settlement system, such as kill sites or resource procurement sites, would have different locational criteria. Similarly chronological differences may affect locational criteria. However, due to data and time limitations, most inductive models rely on a "universal" modeling approach. Another confounding problem with inductive models is that successful predictions cannot be explained (Sebastian and Judge, 1988: 5).

Inductive modeling has also been criticized on the basis of the statistical methods employed and whether those statistical methods accurately can predict human behaviour (Wheatley 1996). An experiment was conducted on lithic density data from Stonehenge using linear multiple regression in order to see if it correctly predicted the lithic densities across the Stonehenge landscape (Wheatley, 1996: 287). Only about 25% of the data was properly predicted. Therefore, Wheatley (1996) questions whether linear regression is appropriate in complex cultural landscapes.

The only predictive modeling done in the boreal forest of Canada so far is the work of the CARP project, which created an inductive model for the boreal forest region near Thunder Bay, Ontario (Dalla Bona, 1994a, Dalla Bona, 1994b, Hamilton et al., 1994, Hamilton and Larcombe, 1994, Larcombe, 1994). Hamilton (e.g. Hamilton, 2000) states that predictive modeling offers a cost-effective solution to conventional reconnaissance techniques. However, there is no consensus as to how APM might be implemented and how its predictive strength might be measured (Hamilton, 2000: 43), especially in the light of our inadequate knowledge about settlement patterns in the region. Despite these concerns and limitations, there is much that can be accomplished through the adoption of inductive models.
Despite the various criticisms of inductive modeling techniques, there is a substantial and undeniable success rate in using inductive models to predict archaeological site locations. This success is reflected in the fact that inductive models are so widely adopted by the cultural resource management industry.

2.2 Deductive Modeling

The basis of deductive modeling is *a priori* archaeological or anthropological knowledge, such as a theory of general human behaviour (Kamermans and Wansleeben, 1999: 225, Kohler, 1999: 37). While this type of model is cited as a more powerful method, it is less frequently employed than inductive techniques (Kamermans and Wansleeben, 1999: 225) due to the complexities in the modeling process. To be considered deductive, a model must have the following set of characteristics: a decision making mechanism for establishing site location, as well as an understanding of the ends of the decision making process (a general theory of human behaviour); 2) specified variables affecting locational decisions (variables appropriate for evaluation of the theory); and 3) the capacity to be operationalized (Kohler and Parker, 1986: 432). Deductive models are applicable to any situation characterized by a specified set of cultural system and ecosystem variables (Sebastian and Judge, 1988: 7), meaning that they are more general than inductive models. The greatest challenge of deductive models is that they are extremely difficult to create and to validate (Sebastian and Judge, 1988: 8).

Since they are based on a general theory of human behaviour, deductive models are more effective in explaining why sites are located where they are; however, they have received little attention in archaeology, probably due to the difficulty in operationalizing these types of models (Dalla Bona, 1994a). It is difficult in the contemporary archaeological literature to even find examples of models that might be considered deductive.

2.3 Methodological Considerations for Models

Predictive modeling creates two types of error: wasteful and gross (Altschul, 1988: 62). When a site is predicted but does not exist, it is a wasteful error (Altschul, 1988: 62). When a location is predicted as not containing sites, but does in fact contain (a) site(s), it is a gross error (Altschul, 1988: 62). While both types of error should be minimized, it is more costly to make a gross error then a wasteful one in terms of protecting heritage resources (Altschul, 1988: 62). In practical terms, it is often difficult to avoid wasteful errors. Many land parcel units identified in predictive models as being of high archaeological potential do not contain sites. As the amount of wasteful error grows, the probability of making gross errors decreases, and vice versa (Altschul, 1988: 62). While too much wasteful error calls the credibility or utility of the model into question, gross errors should be minimized to the greatest extent.

Different types of sites may be associated with different sets of variables (Rose and Altschul, 1988: 205). Therefore, the number of axes into which to divide the data, in order to examine temporal, functional and spatial differences is an important question (Kincaid, 1988: 557, Rose and Altschul, 1988). However, the question remains whether or not adding a high level of detail provides a significant advantage. In his study of Iroquoian villages, Hasenstab (1996: 230) considers three axes of variation: 1) functional (villages versus campsites); 2) temporal (five occupation periods); and 3) spatial (three physiographic/cultural zones). These axes were analyzed on the basis of three classes of environmental data: 1) those related to hunting territories; 2) those related to maize horticulture; and 3) those influencing trade, especially canoe routes (Hasenstab, 1996: 230). Hasenstab (1996) found that the data and methods return only inconclusive answers as to the advantage of making these divisions. However, Hasenstab (1996: 238) also argues that his resultsm may be hard to evaluate, since such as autocorrelation, may be confusing the picture (Hasenstab, 1996: 238).

A number of concerns are expressed in relation to the usefulness of predictive modeling in archaeological research. One concern is the accuracy of site locational data (Duncan and Beckman, 2000: 55, Ebert, 2000, Dalla Bona, 1994a: 29), because sites have been recorded through time by archaeologists with varying accuracy. Another basic concern is the accuracy of the environmental data set (Duncan and Beckman, 2000: 55, Ebert, 2000), as differing data sets are created at different levels of resolution and accuracy. Furthermore, the definition of the categories of archaeological potential is rarely explicitly stated in modeling reports (Dalla Bona, 1994a: 15), making it difficult to evaluate the model results.

2.4 Extending the Application of Inductive Modeling

The traditional inductive model relies on a handful of environmental variables, notably slope, aspect and distance to water as core variables. Other variables may be included, but the core rarely changes. However, it is obvious that these factors might only have a small role to play in locational decisions. Archaeologists have been slow to extend the list of model variables to include other environmental variables or even cultural data. This failure is one of the areas which must be addressed by archaeologists to make predictive modeling more robust.

Inductive modeling allows wide latitude as to which environmental variables can be employed. For example, Allen (1996) chooses climatic variables in order to predict the location of Iroquoian horticultural villages. The predictive variables included in this study included: 1) average length of the frost-free season; 2) the mean temperature during the May-September growing season; and 3) mean precipitation during the growing season (Allen, 1996: 203). Allen's study is an example of how archaeologists might move away from the traditional limited set of variables to employing a wider set of environmental variables in their predictions.

Viewsheds have also been used in a predictive capacity. Viewsheds are created in GIS, through algorithms that calculate what aspects of the landscape would be visible from a given point. The calculation is done through the DEM and is based on differences in height of the land. Pre-contact hunters in the Great Lakes area may have been locating themselves to observe caribou migrations (Krist and Brown, 1994: 1130). A cost surface was created to simulate possible caribou migrations paths (Krist and Brown, 1994). Based on these data, (Krist and Brown, 1994: 1133) predict that hunters located themselves in sheltered areas, close to look-out points for observing migration. This model provides important information about Paleo-Indian and Early Archaic sites in the region (Krist and Brown, 1994: 1135); however, the authors felt that better data regarding caribou migration was necessary to fully evaluate the predictive power of this model (Krist and Brown, 1994: 1135).

2.5 Cultural Land-Use Data and Predictive Modeling

The focus of inductive modeling has traditionally been the correlation of environmental variables with archaeological site location, but the role of social, ideological and political factors has held little importance in the prediction of site locations (Weimer, 1995: 91). Some effort has been made in a few projects to rectify this situation, but little published work exists to guide archaeologists wishing to incorporate these data into their modeling processes. While a large body of ethnographic data is available, it has received limited use. Dalla Bona and Larcombe (1996) introduce an ethnographically reconstructed seasonal round of boreal forest hunter-gatherers into their inductive model of archaeological site locations. One of the reasons for their choice of ethnographic data is the known importance of resources of social or spiritual significance in the study region (Dalla Bona and Larcombe, 1996: 254). From the ethnographic data, they were able to create a series of land-use models, which were coded for inclusion in the predictive model (Dalla Bona and Larcombe, 1996). They argue that their model benefits from the inclusion of ethnographic information, as it included variables that would not have been accessible through traditional environmental predictive models. Stancic and Kvamme (1999) also incorporate what they term "social variables" into their analysis of hillfort locations. Four social variables were employed in their analysis: 1) distance between hillforts, 2) intervisibility; 3) distance from the sea and 4) location of long barrows (Stancic and Kvamme, 1999: 234). In this study, distance between hillforts represents security, as does distance to the ocean. These variables are not employed as if they were environmental predictors; instead they represent cultural preferences, where hillforts were located a considerable distance from the coast for defensive reasons (Stancic and Kvamme, 1999: 234). This approach works well in its context, but it obviously has little applicability to pre-contact hunter-gatherers of the boreal forest, since permanent constructions like hillforts were not employed. Predictive models based solely on environmental considerations do seem to predict the settlement patterns of hunter-gatherers fairly well (Maschner, 1996: 176), but when more complex socio-political forms are examined, such as the tribes of the Northwest coast of Canada or Bronze Age Britain, the predictions do not seem to work as well. This phenomenon is likely due to the fact that complex social systems do not employ the same adaptive strategies as mobile foraging systems, since political decisions and interactions have more of an impact on settlement patterns (Maschner, 1996: 178). In later periods of Northwest coast prehistory, for example, there is a shift in settlement patterning, from a pattern related primarily to the distribution of key resources to one related to defensibility and the creation of larger corporate entities (Maschner, 1996: 187). Maschner (1996: 187) sees this in evolutionary terms as a shift from economic maximization to political maximization. It is clear from these few studies that cultural or social factors can play an important role in making predictions, despite the paucity of examples of their use. However, most of the use of cultural information has been in areas with more complex socio-political systems, such as the aforementioned studies by Maschner (1996) and Stancic and Kvamme (1999).

Except for the work done by Dalla Bona and Larcombe (1996), little has been done with cultural data in the context of North American archaeology. In the context of North American pre-contact archaeology, these types of cultural data can be collected from a wide variety of sources, such as ethnographic data, ethnohistoric data or interviews with Elders of a First Nations community. These data may be broadly classified as traditional land-use information.

2.5.1 Cultural Data in the Manitoba Model Forest (MbMF)

Traditional land use information can effectively be divided into two categories. The first category is the identification of specific resources used. The second is the strategy and behaviours surrounding the use of those resources. The sources of data for these two categories included published ethnographic, ethnohistoric and archaeological records, wildlife and botany data and oral reports from land and resource users from communities, like the Hollow Water First Nation (Manitoba, Canada), consulted in this research.

The inclusion of cultural data in a model has many ramifications that require some consideration. The cultural data used in this research are available from published sources concerning historic and recent historic land use information gathered by Petch and Larcombe (1998). This information was used to identify locations in the study area (MbMF) that were used recently and historically by both First Nations people and other resource users. From these reports, Petch et al (2000) identified nine significant cultural variables including: earth resources, Aboriginal ceremonial sites, local resources, trails and cabin, industrial, fur trade, vegetation, faunal, place names and pictures. Earth resources are geological features of the environment which were available as raw materials for the inhabitants of the region. Local resources data are a fairly amorphous class of land use data and actually cross-cuts several classes of data. This class included any resources that were located close to places that were identified by local residents as habitation sites. A category for pictures was identified so that pictorial information from historic sources and archaeological site documentation could be included, although for the study area for this research there were no pictures available in this category. Each of these cultural features represents a contemporary or historic reality and cannot therefore be treated as a proxy variable. The location of an historic trapper's cabin or a fur trade post, for example, are indicative of certain types of activities at specific locations on the landscape. The cultural model makes the assumption that there may be a correlation between historic or recent historic features and land use in the pre-contact past. Resources such as lithic sources, wild rice lakes, and medicinal plants are important features of contemporary and past land use, but their use does not necessarily leave an archaeological footprint. Nonetheless, the potential association of such cultural aspects of the landscape with habitation areas that are archaeologically visible make them important cultural variables.

2.5.2 Cultural Versus Archaeological Significance

One of the greatest challenges in using cultural data is to make a distinction between cultural relevance and archaeological relevance. The bulk of the cultural data held by the project comes from a previous MbMF project (Petch and Larcombe, 1998), which identified the locations of ethnographically known natural resources, as well as resources that may have been known to the pre-contact inhabitants of a region.

Attempts to define/explain, compare and contrast the concepts of cultural and archaeological relevance are not meant to belittle or denigrate the importance of either category of information. Obviously, all of these data hold a level of cultural significance but not all loci of cultural significance will have archaeological visibility. Conversely, not all archaeologically visible resources were known to people in the past. Consideration of archaeological significance is an attempt to understand the possible visibility of cultural activities in the archaeological record. For instance, several wild rice gathering loci are identified in the land-use data, making these areas of high cultural significance. However, the wild rice collection process will have extremely low archaeological visibility, since the actual rice gathering took place from canoes and therefore would leave no land-based. To further complicate matters, one must consider how these transient activities (from the point-of-view of the archaeological record) would have influenced site location. While pre-contact inhabitants may or may not have camped immediately adjacent to lakes containing wild rice, it is conceivable they would have preferred areas that were easily accessible to resources such as wild rice, and would have located next to a lake with wild rice in preference to a lake which did not. Beyond the consideration of a single resource like wild rice, if a number of resources could be accessed from a particular location, fish or moose for example, such a location would have been highly attractive.

2.5.3 Temporal and Spatial Considerations with Cultural Data

Cultural data in general, and the cultural data collected for this project specifically, provide a number of spatial, temporal and spatio-temporal considerations which must be dealt with in order to successfully employ them in an APM context. Spatially, what elements can be used to represent the locations of some of these entities? Conceivably, cultural data can be represented as any of the geographic entities that are common in GIS – points, lines or polygons. Data collected for this project was distilled to point-location data by the data collectors. There is also a question of how accurately this sensitive cultural data should be represented. Few First Nations communities would be prepared to have traditional land use areas described in great detail, especially the location of sacred sites. A final problem concerns the fact that traditional land use information must take into account both mappable and non-mappable variables. Non-mappable data includes information that may be highly ephemeral, such as the locations of blueberry patches, or may not have quantifiable aspects that can be mapped. Although by its nature a GIS based archaeological model seeks to define each variable as a geographic entity, considering the effective inclusion of relevant but non-mappable information lends explanatory strength.

Temporally, there is the issue of how deep into the pre-contact era the cultural data are applicable. Can they be extended only into the Late Pre-Contact period, or do they represent deeper patterns in time that have longer-standing cultural value? There is likely no easy answer to this question, but it must be considered on a case-by-case basis. Furthermore, not all types of cultural data will share the same time depth. Hamilton (2000: 47) argues that the ethnographic record of the Algonkian speaking peoples of the boreal forest likely only extends at best to the beginning of the mid-19th century; although, the findings of this research indicate that this argument may not be completely valid for the MbMF.

Finally, in terms of spatio-temporal concerns, the question of how long a particular area of cultural significance remains stable must be considered. For instance, wild rice collection areas may be declared good areas if they represent areas with reasonably reliable harvests over a period of time in recent memory. Have these areas always been good rice harvesting locations or have similar areas existed in different locations in deeper time?

These are obviously very serious considerations to take into account when including cultural data in APM. Clearly, these questions are not easily answered and possibly are not answerable. As a precaution, this research has taken a conservative view and restricted modeling with this data to the Woodland period.

2.6 Simulation

An alternative approach to predictive modeling is currently being explored in many new studies: simulation. A simulation model is a simplified representation of reality (Chadwick, 1979: 237). It is not a snapshot of the reality it seeks to represent, but it seeks to represent the processes involved in its evolution, either through description or explanation (Chadwick, 1979: 237).

Advocates of simulation call it a "poor man's systems theory" (Aldenderfer, 1991: 195) because it is able to explore in an efficient manner human behaviours that may be related to the creation of the archaeological record. Detractors see simulation as game play, or more cynically, as a method that may be manipulated to answer any question a researcher may have, without having any theoretical rigour or even plausibility (Aldenderfer, 1991: 195). A middle ground exists, for those archaeologists who believe simulation is a useful tool, as long as it is used carefully, and that any limitations are acknowledged (Aldenderfer, 1991: 195). At their base, simulations must have three parts: 1) a mathematical, logical algorithmic or quantitative model that describes some real world system (the real-world system is referred to as the simuland and the model is called the conceptual model); 2) a conceptual model, which is translated into some format which is compatible with a computer; and 3) behaviours, which are explored through time by the model (*i.e.* the model is a dynamic representation of some system under a given set of operating conditions) (Aldenderfer, 1991: 197).

Simulation has generally been employed in three ways by archaeologists: 1) as a tool to force clear thinking in the formulation of a problem; 2) as an experimental laboratory; or 3) to generate data (Aldenderfer, 1991: 211). The advantage of simulation is that the models emphasize dynamic processes, distributed processes and relationships among agents, which are not the case with traditional analyses (Kohler, 1999: 2). Simulation cannot reveal the entire process of human experience, but, it does allow researchers access to portions of it (Kohler, 1999: 3).

A specialized form of simulation, which has received more attention of late, is agent-based simulation. Agent-based simulation allows the creation of landscapes that can be wholly imaginary or can be representative of real-world situations (or aspects thereof) (Dean et al., 1999: 179). Agents can be modified to represent important features of individuals or social units, such as households (Dean et al., 1999: 179). The way that agents behave in relation to each other or the environment can be governed by anthropologically validated rules (Dean et al., 1999: 180). In this sense, simulations are specialized cases of deductive models, but they use a special set of techniques to create the deductive model.

A popular area in which to attempt agent-based simulation is the American Southwest, specifically the area occupied by the Anasazi in between 900 and 1300 A.D. Studies in this area include simulation of farming (e.g.Dean et al., 1999, Van West, 1994) and settlement patterns (e.g.Kohler et al., 1999). Simulation has also been employed to examine the relationship between changes in settlement patterns and changes in the pattern of raiding in the Oaxaca Valley (Reynolds, 1999), Aztec settlement patterns and distribution networks (Ruggles and Church, 1996), and Mesolithic foragers in Scotland (Lake, 1999). All of these simulations have met with mixed degrees of success, but they allow archaeologists to examine patterns that would not be otherwise accessible for study. Two of the great problems of these simulations are that they frequently do not employ explicit theoretical models nor are they georeferenced. Most commonly, the base of the simulation is a common-sense model that either assumes or implies optimality. The lack of georeferencing, meaning an explicit delineation of the simulation area in a coordinate system, often means that these simulations are not available for the types of manipulation done in GIS. This problem also means that simulation predictions are not comparable with more traditional types of predictive modeling.

Lake (1999) demonstrates the use of a simulation module for the GRASS GIS system, called MAGICAL (Multi-Agent Geographically Informed Computer Analysis), which avoids both of the aforementioned drawbacks of simulation models. MAGICAL was specifically designed for hunter-gatherer studies so it reflects an emphasis on mobility, subsistence and rational decision making (Lake, 1999: 108). The simulation is based on optimal foraging rules created in the parameters given to each agent. Each agent in MAGICAL has its own set of variables, affected by its own life history (Lake, 1999: 110). This means that the system being modeled is an adaptive system, where the agent can learn from its actions, changing its strategy in response to previous successful actions (Gilbert, 1999: 364). Using an evolutionary-ecological paradigm, agents can be given a user-specified genotype (Lake, 1999: 111), which can allow each agent to have different characteristics, thus mimicking the diversity that might be found in a real-world social system. The core of MAGICAL is an event scheduler, which receives requests from agents to perform certain actions and grants permission at appropriate times (Lake, 1999: 111). MAGICAL differs from many other simulations because its spatial database allows all actions in MAGICAL simulations to be georeferenced (Lake, 1999: 112). In the only test of MAGICAL to date, foragers were sent out foraging for hazelnuts on the island of Islay in Scotland (Lake, 1999: 117). The results were somewhat problematic, because simulation predictions of artifact discard patterns and the settlement patterns did not mesh well with the known archaeological record (Lake, 1999). It is thought, therefore, that foraging for hazelnuts was not a major determinant of Mesolithic land use on Islay (Lake, 1999: 137).

It is clear that simulation offers a new and exciting approach to predicting human behaviour, and agent-based modeling gives archaeologist a powerful new tool to employ. However, there are serious questions to be posed in relation to simulation and its operation before simulation becomes a regular tool of the cultural resource manager. Anthropologically-grounded simulations, such as MAGICAL, might indicate the future rise of deductive modeling. Until that time comes, archaeologists need to continue exploring new ways to improve inductive models, such as through the examination of new predictive variables.

Chapter 3 Optimal Foraging Theory

3.0 Optimal Foraging Theory

Optimal foraging theory (OFT) grows out of a number of models, adopted from biology in anthropology and archaeology in the 1960's and 1970's which rely on optimization logic as their foundation. Optimization models are explicitly attempting to define human behaviour, or some aspect thereof, in terms of the optimization of a particular function, given certain constraints (Jochim (1983: 157-158). There are a number of attractive features of the approach. First, optimization attempts to be unbiased and allows for cross-cultural comparisons (Jochim, 1983: 158). The use of optimization logic allows for precise measurement of changes in environmental variables (Jochim, 1983: 158). While optimization models can be complex mathematically, they are a response to the complexity of the real world (Jochim, 1983: 158). Finally, archaeologists can use optimization models to test subsistence and settlement predictions against evidence in the archaeological record (Jochim, 1983: 158). One such optimization model is OFT. OFT is based on two Neo-Darwinian assumptions (Keene, 1983: 140). The first Neo-Darwinian assumption is that natural selection and competition are an outgrowth of finite resources, both natural and reproductive (Keene, 1983: 140). The second of these assumptions is that greater efficiency in life goals is rewarded by greater fitness (Keene, 1983: 140).

Optimal foraging theory is not explicitly used in the modeling of hunter-gatherer site locations in this research. In this case, OFT is being used as the theoretical basis for the economic variables in the creation of models. The assumption is made that if foragers in the boreal forest study area are, in fact, foraging optimally, then site locations should reflect that optimality.

It is often said of hunter-gatherers that they maintain an equilibrium relationship with their prey, sometimes managing herds, even if at an unconscious level, to ensure that prey is not seriously depleted (Alvard, 1995: 789). However, the management of prey species is not universal and equilibrium can be achieved through other methods, such as mobility after prey depletion. The use of environmental or conservation principles to explain this phenomenon is a controversial idea (Alvard, 1995). Microeconomic theory, such as the Law of Diminishing Returns, may better explain such economic behaviour.

OFT is a body of theory, originally formulated in biology (McArthur and Pianka, 1966), but ultimately rooted in microeconomic principles, which has been adopted into anthropological research. OFT provides a method for the analysis and prediction of economic activity based on a well-established set of principles. The underlying logic of optimal foraging theory is hunter-gatherer economics can be understood on the basis of a cost-benefit analysis (Hawkes et al., 1982: 379, Alvard, 1995: 795, Bettinger, 1987).

OFT consists of a series of models (examined below) that can be used to examine the selection of individual food resources, where and for how long a forager should exploit these items and where foragers might locate themselves in relation to these resources. In general, the currency used to measure energy in the OFT models is calories, because activities can be broken down into energy expenditures, and food consumption can be measured by caloric gain (Jochim, 1979: 90-91).

3.1 OFT Models

Optimal foraging models are summarized in Table 1, giving data for each of the models on goals, the domain in which choices are made, the criteria and constraints. OFT models include: the Diet Breadth Model, the Patch Choice Model, the Marginal Value Theorem and central place foraging. Each of these models and how they operate is discussed below.

Table 1: Summary of the Goals, Domains of Choice, Benefits and Constraints of OFT (Smith 1983)

Decision Category	Strategic Goal	Domain of Choice	Cost-Benefit Criteria	Some Major Constraining Variables
Diet breadth	Optimal set of resource types which to exploit	Which types to harvest, once encountered	Return per unit handling time for each type, overall return on foraging (incl. search time)	Search and pursuit abilities of the forager
Diet breadth w/ nutrient constraints	Same as above	Which and how many of each prey type to harvest	Minimum cost for meeting nutritional requirements	Nutrient requirements, abundance of prey, procurement costs
Patch Choice	Optimal array of habitats to exploit	Which set of patches to visit	Average rate of return with patch types and average over all patches (incl. travel time between patches)	Efficiency of ranking patch types, travel time between patches
Time allocation (MVT)	Optimal pattern of time allocated to alternatives (patches, etc.)	Time spent foraging in each alternative	Marginal return rate for each alternative, av. rate of return for entire set	Resource richness, depletion rates for each alternative
Settlement pattern	Optimal location of home base for foraging efficiency	Settlement location of each foraging unit (individual or family)	Mean travel costs, and/or search costs per unit harvest	Spatiotemporal dispersion and predictability of major resources, effects of co-operation and competition

3.1.1 Diet Breadth Model

The diet breadth model defines what set of food items foragers should eat, based on costs and returns of each particular food resource. The diet breadth model predicts hunting and gathering activities as food items are encountered and decisions are made as to whether to acquire the food resource or to forgo the item, continuing the food quest (Hawkes and O'Connell, 1992: 63, Hill, 1988: 161, Kaplan and Hill, 1992: 169, Smith, 1983: 627). Foragers can be generalists (consuming a diverse set of food types) or specialists (consuming a restricted range of food types) (Winterhalder, 1981b: 23). Foragers with a high search/pursuit cost ratio will tend towards a generalized diet breadth, whereas a low search/pursuit cost ratio implies a specialist diet breadth (Winterhalder, 1981b: 25). While the model considers the amount of time involved in handling the food resource (*i.e.* pursuit, capture and processing) it does not consider the amount of time engaged in search (Hawkes and O'Connell, 1992: 63). Food resources are ranked based on energy expenditure in their acquisition against the caloric benefits of consuming the food resource (Hawkes and O'Connell, 1992: 63). High ranked resources minimize the amount of energy expended in acquisition against the amount of energy gained by their consumption (Hawkes and O'Connell, 1992: 64). The model has three implications: 1) individual food items will always either be exploited or ignored; 2) the caloric value of an item is not the sole determinant of exploitation, other costs (*i.e.* search, pursuit and handling time) are factored-in as well; and 3) exploitation does not depend upon the abundance of the food resource, but on the abundance of other more profitable alternatives (Kaplan and Hill, 1992: 171-172). It is assumed that: 1) searching for and handling food items are mutually exclusive activities; 2) prey are encountered sequentially and randomly, but in proportion to abundance in the environment; 3) prey types are uniformly distributed; 4) foragers have no impact on resource distribution or abundance; 5) forgone pursuit does not involve any handling time and does not subtract from search time; and 6) the forager knows, through past experience, average energy returns and handling costs for each food resource item (Kaplan and Hill, 1992: 170, Smith, 1983: 628).

Diet breadth can be represented graphically. The graph shown in Figure 1 is a graph of diet breadth. On the Y-axis is time. On the X-axis are the various food resources ranked from lowest to highest handling costs, usually measured in energy expenditure. The optimal diet is determined by the point of intersection of search time and handling time, as shown by point A in Figure 1. Any resource to the left of the point of intersection should be included in an optimal diet. Items that are lower ranked (*i.e.* to the right of point A in Figure 1) should only be consumed in cases where higher ranked items are not available (Bettinger, 1980). This model also predicts that as overall abundance of resources decreases, the number of items included in an optimal diet will increase (Bettinger, 1980), although high-ranked items should never drop out of the diet, as long as they are available (Hawkes and O'Connell, 1992). In fact, the diet breadth model provides the only source of information that shows how foragers might respond to changes in resource distribution and density (Winterhalder et al., 1988).

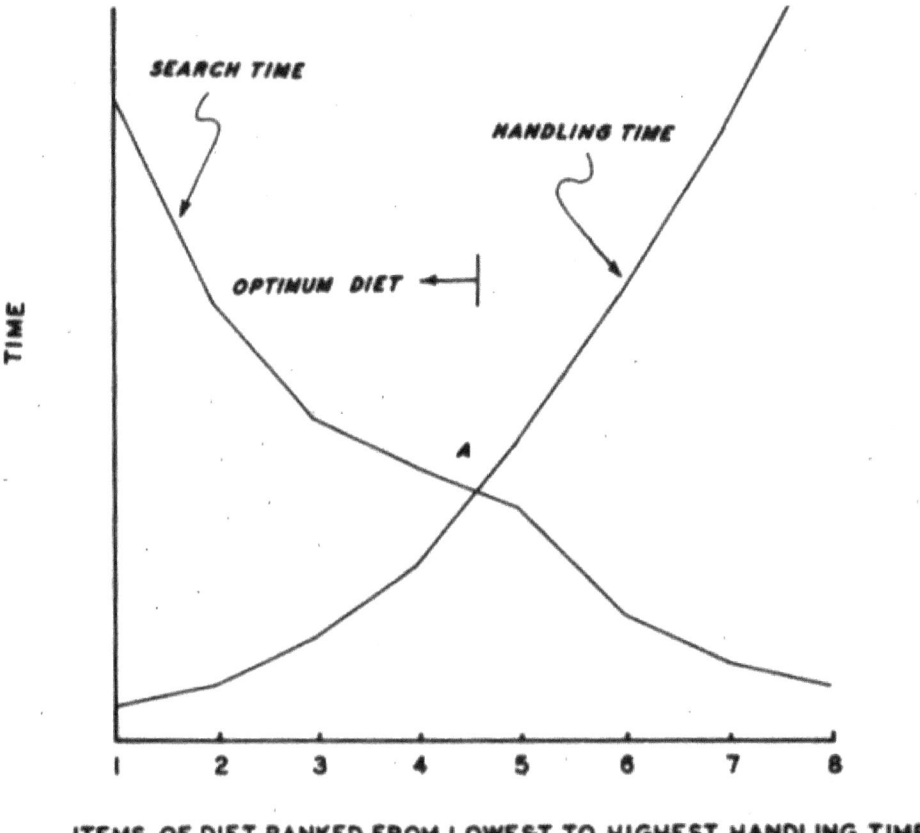

Figure 1: Graphical Determination of Diet Breadth
(Bettinger 1980)

The model can be explained in basic terms: a forager should stop the search for food resources and invest the handling time necessary to pursue and eat a food item, only if, on average, the forager cannot increase their food intake by foregoing the encountered food item and by moving on and encountering a more valuable food type (Kurland and Beckerman, 1985). However, foragers should always stop searching when encountering high-ranked items (Hawkes and O'Connell, 1992). Total search time is clearly correlated to the relative density of the high-ranked items in the patch (Martin, 1985). This model is obviously extremely simplistic. Not only does it assume that resources are equally distributed across space, but it cannot account for time and energy needed to exploit resources (Bettinger, 1991). This weakness has been rectified through the addition of the patch choice model and the Marginal Value Theorem to OFT.

3.1.2 Patch Choice Model

The patch choice model (PCM) accounts for the fact that resources are not distributed uniformly in an environment, rather they are differentially distributed (Hawkes et al., 1982: 391, Kaplan and Hill, 1992: 178). A patch is an ecological construct, which is problem- and organism-defined, based on the behaviour, size, mobility and habits of the population of interest (Winterhalder, 1994). This model is in a similar vein to the diet breadth model, in that it calculates the optimum point beyond which declines in yield per unit time spent foraging in patches no longer compensates for traveling between patches (Smith, 1983: 631). An important aspect of this model is the concept of grain size. Grain size is determined through a relative measurement of patch sizes within the environment or through the assessment of behaviour of the forager (Winterhalder, 1981b: 23). Foragers who organize their activities in order to exploit patches in proportion to their occurrence in the environment are acting in what is referred to as a fine-grained manner (Winterhalder, 1981b: 23). Conversely, foragers who spend a disproportionate amount of time in certain patches are acting in a coarse-grained manner (Winterhalder, 1981b: 23). Fine-grain foragers will tend towards generalized use of habitats, whereas coarse-grain foragers will tend towards specialized use of patches (Winterhalder, 1981b: 29). However, even advocates of OFT note that patchiness is a difficult variable to quantify (Cashdan, 1992: 242).

3.1.3 Marginal Value Theorem

The patch choice model provides no measure of how long a forager should spend in a patch before abandoning it or how a forager might deplete the resources in the patch (Smith, 1983: 631). The Marginal Value Theorem (MVT) accounts for these factors. The MVT takes the set of patches utilized and determines the optimal pattern of time allocation (Smith, 1983: 631). As the net rate of harvest for a particular patch becomes depressed, the model predicts the point at which foragers should leave

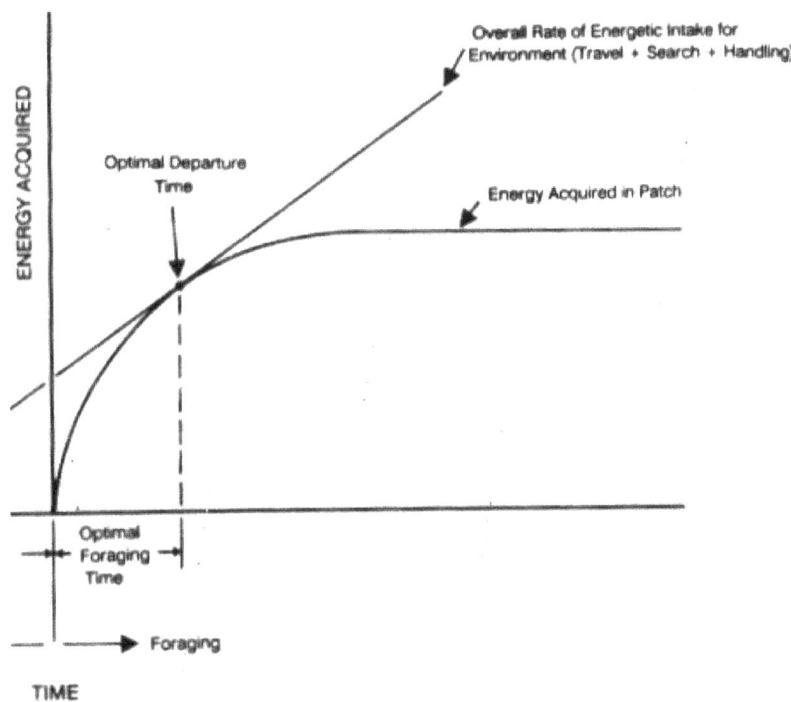

**Figure 2: Graphic Representation of MVT
(Bettinger 1991)**

the patch and search for a patch that is not depleted (Winterhalder, 1981a: 69). A forager should abandon a patch when the marginal capture rate drops below the average capture rate for the habitat (Winterhalder, 1981b: 28), as is shown graphically in Figure 2.

In this model, energy acquired is represented on the Y-axis, and time on the X-axis. Two curves are represented, one curve representing the overall rate of return from the environment (measured in energy acquired) and the second curve representing the energy acquired in the patch. At the point where the energy level falls below the intake for the environment at the margin, the forager should abandon the patch. This depression of energy intake occurs due to a variety of factors: 1) the forager depletes the resources in the locale, 2) the forager exploits the most accessible resources first and then must work harder to exploit less accessible resources (i.e. depletes the readily available food items harvested first and then must work harder to find what is left of that food item), or 3) the forager may force prey to either emigrate or conceal themselves (Winterhalder, 1981a: 69). The largest problem encountered with the MVT is it only accounts for time spent within a patch, and travel time to and from patches is not taken into account. Central place foraging has been proposed to account for this variable.

3.1.4 Central Place Foraging

Central place foraging factors travel costs to and from patches into the cost of foraging for food resources; however, the model recognizes that human foragers do not generally live in or at the patches that they tend to exploit. Humans tend to return to a central place (i.e. a base camp) from which they make daily foraging trips (Kaplan and Hill, 1992). These costs can be conceptualized as a continuum, at one end foragers leave camp, engage in a random search and return to camp with the exploited food resources. At the opposite end of the scale, the forager leaves the camp with a specific resource targeted in advance (Kaplan and Hill, 1992: 184). The amount of time that will be spent traveling to a patch depends on the amount of energy that can be extracted from that patch, as well as the handling time for the resource once in the patch (Bettinger, 1991). Central place foraging assumes that the camp should be located at a spot that minimizes travel time to and from foraging locations with food items of interest (Cashdan, 1992: 250).

The central place model can also be shown graphically, as shown in Figure 3. In Figure 3, the upper curve represents the expected energy that can be gained from traveling to the patch of interest. The lower curve represents the expected search time in the patch. If the points on the axes of expected energy and search time are intersected, and a tangent is drawn through that intersection to the X axis, it will indicate the time that the forager will be prepared to travel in order to exploit the patch (Bettinger, 1991). Time is represented on the X axis on either side of its intersection with the Y axis. Time on the right side of the axis represents the foraging time (i.e. the MVT) and time on the left side of the axis represents the amount of time that a forager will be prepared to travel to a patch.

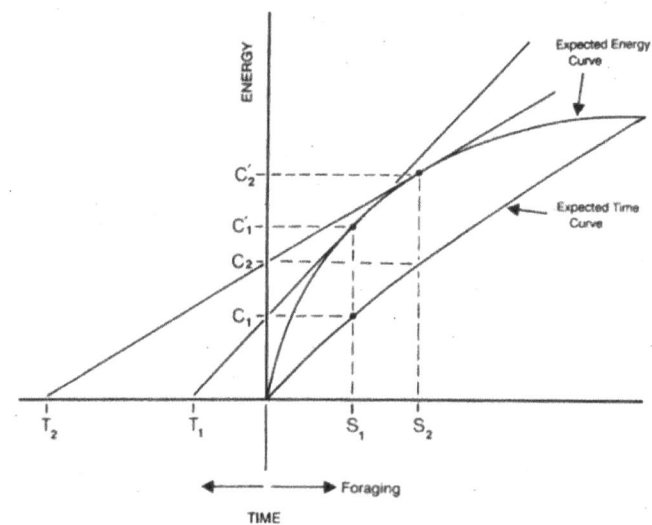

Figure 3: Graphical determination of travel times
for Central Place Foraging (Bettinger 1991)

3.1.5 Anthropological Applications of Optimal Foraging Theory

Anthropologically, OFT has been widely applied to both contemporary and past human societies. Contemporary foraging groups examined have included the Aché of Paraguay (diet breadth) (Hawkes et al., 1982) and an Amazonian group, the Piro (diet breadth) (Alvard, 1995). OFT has also been used with non-foraging groups, including: the decisions of cattle herdsmen in Burkina Faso (patch choice) (De Boer and Prins, 1989), the Machiguenga of Peru, a horticultural population (diet breadth) (Keegan, 1986) and the fishing strategies of a Brazilian community (patch choice) (Begossi, 1992). OFT has been quite successful in predicting human behaviour, at least according its advocates.

Archaeologically, OFT has seen much less application. Applications of OFT archaeologically have included: the foraging of hominids (diet breadth) (Kurland and Beckerman, 1985), California aboriginal groups and the over-exploitation of local resources (diet breadth) (Broughton, 1994b, Broughton, 1994a: 372, Broughton, 1997) and the Late Pleistocene in Canada (diet breadth) (Zutter, 1989). One of the greatest problems of the archaeologist is the knowledge of exactly what resources were available to the forager, especially in deep time where palaeoenvironmental reconstructions have not been completed.

3.2 Criticisms and Modifications of Optimal Foraging Theory

OFT has faced the scrutiny of a number of critics who have discovered and identified several shortcomings in basic OFT models. Since then, however, OFT advocates have offered solutions to these problems and have found ways to improve the basic models. Bettinger (1987: 104) argues, though, that much of the criticism is rhetorical rather than substantive, mostly deriving from humanistic philosophies that reject simple explanations of complex behaviour.

The criticisms of OFT can be broken into two types – those that are critical of the model and what it fails to account for in economic terms, and those that criticize the model based on mainly cultural terms. The two greatest criticisms of OFT are in regards to economic aspects of the model itself. They are: 1) the use of the optimization logic and 2) the use of energy, specifically calories, as the currency in which optimal foraging is computed. The model has also been criticized on economic grounds because it fails to account for resource fluctuations. Culturally, the model has been criticized for not taking into account many aspects of human cultural behaviour, such as the sexual division of labour, scheduling, sharing of food and non-economic foraging motivations.

The assumption that foragers consciously optimize their decisions has been questioned (Martin, 1983: 613, Mithen, 1989). There has been discussion as to the exact definition of optimality – whether in energetic, cultural or other terms. It is likely that this confusion about how optimality might be defined is due to a misinterpretation of what optimality truly means. Optimality does not refer to the absolute optimality of a diet or of some other behaviour, but rather refers to relative optimality. Namely, given two alternatives, the forager would choose the better of the two. In the case of OFT, these alternatives are evaluated purely on an economic basis. Martin (1983) argues that, as prey learn to avoid the forager or decline in density, the efficiency of foraging in the patch declines. He argues that, taken literally, OFT stipulates that the forager operates at the highest point on the marginal return curve (Martin, 1983: 613). Therefore, optimization must be defined in terms of the properties of the forager and their environment (Martin, 1985: 649). It has also been suggested that instead of optimization, the goal should be "meliorizing", where foragers are trying to improve upon, and not optimize, current foraging efficiencies (Mithen, 1989: 61). Supporters of OFT counter that optimization logic does not require that the foraging organism be engaged in rational choice or the denial of intentionality; instead, it predicts that selection will favour the best strategy from a defined set of alternatives possible (Broughton and O'Connell, 1999: 154).

While many researchers have employed OFT in the analysis of hunter-gatherer subsistence, concern has been expressed at the idea of using caloric intake alone for the energy currency (Hill, 1988, Jochim, 1979: 91). One of the problems with energy as a currency is the link between energy efficiency and fitness has not been demonstrated (Keene, 1983: 143). It has been argued that there are important reasons for the use of energy as a currency, however. Resource fluctuation must be measured in relation to dietary requirements of the group (Winterhalder, 1981b: 21). That is, energy shortages would have been periodic, but recurrent, problems for hunter-gatherers and would have produced a selection environment favouring efficient foraging (Winterhalder, 1981b: 21). Energy is a clearly amenable currency, which can be quantified and studied (Winterhalder, 1981b: 21). On the other hand, human diets are not based solely on calories but require a balance of nutrients to comprise a sustainable diet (Kaplan and Hill, 1992: 189, Martin, 1983: 619). Advocates of optimal foraging acknowledge this point, but they argue that energy is the most important component of food (Winterhalder, 1981b: 21). Hill (1988: 169) proposes the adoption of indifference curves from biology, which have been used to study alternatives between desirable resources. Indifference curves are based on the assumption that, for any two given desirable resources, any number of different combinations of these resources can define a line of equal satisfaction (Hill, 1988: 170). This line is referred to as an indifference curve, because the consumer should find all choices along the curve indifferent (Hill, 1988: 170). The indifference curves require data on the available income (time, energy and resources to be expended on commodities) and the price of the commodities (Hill, 1988: 172). This type of indifference curve can give OFT models a different approach to measuring efficiency, therefore not depend solely on energy as a measure of efficiency.

OFT has been criticized as being inattentive to the time frame in which foraging occurs (Yesner, 1985). OFT does not take into account any aspect of time, especially seasonality, which can greatly affect the availability of resources. Foraging is assumed to happen in a timeless and unchanging landscape. While patch choice and MVT seem to take into account resource distribution and depletion, they fail to account for resource fluctuations, whether caused by seasonal change or natural disaster (Yesner, 1985: 413).

Failure of OFT to account for various aspects of cultural systems has also been pointed out. For example, sharing of the catch also creates problems for OFT, as the cost-benefit analysis is done strictly for individual hunters (Dwyer, 1985: 243). Therefore, sharing requires that OFT be done at a group level and not at the level of the individual. The possible social motivation to hunt has also been a cultural criticism of the model (Dwyer, 1985: 243). Foraging may be motivated by ceremonial or ritual needs, or any number of non-economic considerations. The counter-argument to this criticism would be simply that it does not matter as to why the foraging was motivated, but only that it happens, whatever the initiating motivation, in an optimal manner.

One of the most common social divisions in hunter-gatherer groups is the division of labour, especially in subsistence activities, between men and women (Jochim, 1988: 130). Jochim (1988: 131) goes so far as to state that men and women occupy separate econiches. Women have different reproductive strategies than men, and to fulfill those adaptive interests the best course is to follow a foraging strategy of their own (Jochim, 1988: 135). If men and women were modeled separately, as Jochim (1988) suggests, the sum of two optimal diet strategies may appear to be suboptimal. However this would enable archaeologists to model the sexual division of labour. He proposes that women should pursue those resources that are of high reliability and men those of low reliability (although, often high return) (Jochim, 1988: 134).

OFT has been criticized for not taking into account either risk or uncertainty, which is clearly a valid criticism of the models. Risk and uncertainty are stochastic processes in evolutionary ecological analysis. That is, the variation of outcomes cannot be controlled by the decision maker (Smith, 1988: 230). Risk is variation in outcome that is associated with decision, whereas uncertainty is the lack of perfect information affecting decision makers (Smith, 1988: 231). There are five ways in which a forager can reduce risk; 1) alter foraging practices (*e.g.* select less risky prey), 2) store resources against resource shortages; 3) exchange resources; 4) pool resources and/or 5) move to a locale with better foraging returns (Smith, 1988: 233). These criticisms of OFT can be accounted for through the use of linear programming, as demonstrated by (Belovsky, 1987, Belovsky, 1988, Keene, 1979, Keene, 1981).

Linear programming provides a minimization-maximization solution to a problem, where certain variables are minimized (*e.g.* risk, time) while some variables are maximized (*e.g.* nutrient intake) (Belovsky, 1987). Linear programming also allows for the addition of constraints, while preserving the basic nature of the OFT models. Constraints can be used to counter most of the above criticisms, including: the expansion of the measures of efficiency beyond energy to include other factors of foods, such as protein or carbohydrate values; the sexual division of labour; and risk and uncertainty.

For example, Belovsky (1987, 1988) modifies the diet breadth model by introducing constraints. The model is constrained by: 1) the amount of each type of food that people can digest given their digestive tract's capacity, the turnover rate of different foods in the digestive tract and the amount of the digestive tract filled by a unit of intake of each food; 2) the amount of each type of food that people can harvest in some foraging period (*e.g.* a day) which is set by climatic and physiological limits to activity, and the rate at which each food can be harvested given its abundance as well as the time required to prepare it for consumption and make tools to harvest it; and 3) the amount of each type of food that must be ingested by people to satisfy their physiological demands for protein and energy, given the digestible protein and energy content of each food (Belovsky, 1988: 331-332). Additional parameters, such as the demography of the foraging population, as well as the prey population, were added in order to improve the overall level of prediction by the OFT models (Belovsky, 1988: 359). It would also be theoretically possible to add many other constraints, as long as they are in some way quantifiable, to an OFT linear programming model (Belovsky, 1988). Overall, Belovsky (1987, 1988) argues in favour of using OFT, especially when modified with constraints.

These modifications, such as linear programming, indifference curves and separate OFT analyses for men and women, have been contested by advocates of OFT. They argue that the promised gains in precision and realism may in fact be illusory (Smith, 1991: 49-50). For example, the precise level of nutritional needs and the effects of deficiencies in these needs over time are poorly understood (Smith, 1991: 49). Furthermore, it is arguable whether or not a forager makes conscious prey-selection decisions based on the ability of a certain resource to fulfill their calcium or iron requirements, as opposed to a simple understanding that the consumption of a resource will fulfill their hunger (Smith, 1991: 49-50). Even advocates of optimal foraging allow for the fact that in human studies, ecological modeling is only partially reliable outside of a heuristic role (Winterhalder, 1977: 571) due to the fact it is often impossible to collect all of the necessary data that the models require.

There is power to OFT, despite its shortcomings. Its power lies in the fact that it can explain quite complex behaviours in relatively simple terms (Bettinger, 1987: 104). It gives archaeologists a basis for understanding economic decisions by foragers, even if they do not precisely fit the patterns seen.

Chapter 4 Hunter-Gatherers of the Boreal Forest

4.0 Hunter-Gatherers of the Boreal Forest

Hunter-gatherers have been the focus of anthropological study for a number of decades. Since the "Man the Hunter" conferences of the 1960's, the minutia of hunter-gatherer existence have been probed and analyzed. This chapter focuses on one particular aspect of hunter-gatherer studies: settlement patterning and how it affects GIS studies of hunter-gatherers. Since the focus of this research is on the boreal forest region of Manitoba, the following chapter concentrates on ethnography of the boreal forest people (the Ojibway and the Cree).

4.1 Boreal Forest Ethnography

There are several commonalities shared among hunter-gatherer groups of the boreal forest (Simpson, 1999). While cultural patterns of the area are not completely homogeneous throughout the Boreal Forest region, there are distinct commonalities, so groups like the Mistassini of Quebec have taken on similar adaptations as the Ojibway of Manitoba. Hunter-gatherer bands of the Boreal Forest may be viewed as politically autonomous, semi-nomadic bands ranging from thirty to one hundred individuals (Fisher, 1969: 10, Hallowell, 1992: 50).

4.1.1 Boreal Forest Social Organization

There is a tendency to virilocality in boreal forest groups, although in strict terms bands should be considered ambilocal (Fisher, 1969: 10, Martijn and Rogers, 1969: 100-101, Smith, 1981, Rogers, 1969). Bilateral kinship is common and cross-cousin marriage is the preference Fisher (1969: 10-11, Rogers, 1962: B10). The evidence for endo- or exogamy tends to be contradictory. Fisher (1969: 11) states that boreal forest bands were neither endogamous nor exogamous, rather they allowed marriage partners to be chosen from both in and outside the band. Rogers (1962: A22) refers to the Round Lake Ojibwa as endogamous (see also Rogers, 1963a, Hallowell, 1992: 45), and to the Mistassini as showing a preference for marriages between families with territories in close proximity to one another (Rogers, 1963b: 28). Bishop (1974: 55) argues for clan-based exogamy.

In pre-contact times, these kinship features may have been moderated by strong pragmatic considerations, as well as operating at different intensities across the boreal forest (Sieciechowicz, 1986: 192-193).

The regional band, or macroband, was composed of several local bands, or microbands (Rogers, 1969: 22). The regional band rarely assembled as a complete unit in the boreal forest (Rogers, 1969: 22). The basic building block of boreal forest social organization was and is the family hunting band (Fisher, 1969: 14, Speck, 1973: 58, Tanner, 1973: 103, Rogers, 1969: 26), which can be considered as the local band. The family hunting group comprises blood or marriage relatives and their partners, which has the right to hunt, trap and fish in a specific territory bounded by some natural boundary, such as lakes or rivers (Speck, 1973: 59), although this territorial imperative is a controversial idea amongst researchers in the area, as discussed below. The hunting group tends to consist of several family units (Rogers, 1963b: 27, Tanner, 1979: 22, Smith, 1981: 259). It is the hunting group, and not the band, that held right of usufruct, according to Martijn (1969: 98), amongst others. Relations within the hunting group tended to be patrilineal (Rogers, 1969: 26). The hunting group was also vested with the authority to resolve any disputes regarding hunting territories according to Rogers (1963b: 26). The hunting group tended to be lead by an older male, who, along with his family form the core of the group (Rogers, 1963b: 55-57). Other nuclear families, as many as two to four, tend to re-join core groups year-after-year (Rogers, 1963b: 57). The nuclear family, or the household (most often the equivalent of the nuclear family), is the basic social unit (Rogers, 1962: B69, Rogers, 1963b: 30, Bishop, 1974: 56), also forming an important economic unit (Rogers, 1962: B71). The family was lead by the family head, who was an authority and a religious figure responsible for the well-being of the family (Rogers, 1962: B4). All members over approximately the age of eight participated in the economic activities of the family (Rogers, 1962: B71).

4.1.2 Socio-Territorial Organization

There are four general socio-territorial organizations in Northern Ojibwa society: 1) community hunting lands (the total land area) (*i.e.* the regional band); 2) the patronymic territories (lands used by co-residential units); 3) co-residential unit areas (lands used by specific commensal units) (*i.e.* the hunting group or local band); and 4) individual traplines in post-contact period (*i.e.* specific members of a hunting group) (Sieciechowicz, 1986: 188). Leadership at levels higher than the family hunting group tended to be vested in a leader with little power or authority (Rogers, 1969: 40). The leader tended to be a charismatic individual who was thought to have superior spiritual powers, which he used to protect the group (Rogers, 1962: A22). Northern Algonquian groups also had a clan organization, although it seemed to have little importance in political life of the group (Hickerson, 1988: 45). It seems that the clan may have played a greater role in pre-contact times (Hickerson, 1988: 46), and may be even equivalent to pre-contact hunting groups (Bishop, 1974: 7-8).

Territoriality is defined by Bishop (1986: 43) as the "exclusive use by humans of one or more culturally identified and defined resources within a specified area by a specified individual or group." Territoriality is seen as a response to resource fluctuations, where existing resources, such as native copper or beaver, could be exchanged in a predictable fashion for other desired materials (Bishop, 1986: 41). Territoriality can also been seen as a method of resource management, by restricting who has access to the resource and at what times (Bishop, 1986: 44-45). This is an ecological response, helping balance population size and the resources needed to sustain the population (Berkes, 1986: 146). Bishop (1986), among others, argues that Subarctic hunter-gatherers likely practiced neither territoriality or resource management. He draws on several lines of evidence to prove this point. First, Subarctic hunter-gatherers are referred to in the earliest records as being highly mobile, making territorial exclusion impossible (Bishop, 1986: 54). Furthermore, spiritual beliefs of Algonquians included reincarnation, which means that game would be available whenever needed, so long as the hunter treated the animal with respect, thus precluding a need for conservation practices (Bishop, 1986: 55). Therefore Bishop (1986) argues that the more likely system in operation was an allotment system (see also Tanner, 1986: 26-27, Tanner, 1979: 185-186).

Territoriality among the Northern Algonquian is a sophisticated system, which responds to local resource fluctuations. For example, an area can be used intensively until resources are relatively depleted, and then left for a period of time to regenerate (also referred to as rotational hunting) (Craik and Casgrain, 1986: 179, Feit, 1973: 122, Tanner, 1973: 103). Alternatively, exploitation of a resource can be done on a restricted basis each year, leaving sufficient breeding stock for subsequent years (Craik and Casgrain, 1986: 179-180). In times of game shortage or abundance, group fission and fusion served to spread people across the landscape and alleviate some resource stress (Sieciechowicz, 1986: 190, Tanner, 1973: 104).

The idea of territoriality versus usufruct has also been examined in relation to Algonquians (Cooper, 1939, Hallowell, 1992: 45). Usufruct is a limited right of possession (Cooper, 1939: 69). The most dramatic changes in socio-territorial organization of the Northern Algonquians were forced on them by the extermination of the large fauna on which they depended for both subsistence and trade (Bishop, 1972: 65). This forced a dietary switch to small game, which could not support large winter groups and necessitated an increased dependence upon trade goods (Bishop, 1972: 65). Therefore, in the early 1800's a trend was established for bands to split into family units, which spent at least part of the winter in a defined region, leading to the establishment of hunting territories (Bishop, 1972: 65). Berkes (1986: 157) argues against this point of view from an ecological standpoint, stating that territories were likely to appear due to the intensification of resource use, possibly caused by changes in technology and population growth.

4.1.3 The Seasonal Round

The archaeological record of the boreal forest indicates that the settlement pattern of the region consisted of small seasonal habitation sites and associated hunting camps (Dawson, 1981: 81), as well as seasonal aggregation sites. These seasonal habitations tend to be located in areas of greater variety and density of fauna, such as ecotonal boundaries (Dawson, 1981: 81, Tanner, 1979: 36). Water, especially lakes, formed the focus of summer aggregations (Feit, 1969: 34), generally occuring in the shoreline zone (Malasiuk, 1999: 32, Martijn and Rogers, 1969: 98, Clelland, 1966: 69, Rogers, 1963c: 9, Ray, 1974: 37, Tanner, 1979: 37). Mobility was a necessity in order to efficiently exploit the Boreal Forest environment (Martijn and Rogers, 1969: 84, 126, Bishop, 1974: 266). In fact, mobility may even have included exiting the Boreal Forest for the Parklands to the south in certain seasons (Ray, 1974: 44).

The faunal communities of the boreal forest vary in space and time (Bishop, 1972: 59). The Subarctic is characterized by long winters, short summers and a continental climate (Brown and Wilson, 1986: 143). The climate, no doubt had a severe effect on game cycles and the resources that would have been available to the hunter-gatherers (Rogers, 1986: 206). In general, resource productivity can be seen as increasing as one traverses westward from the Labrador Peninsula to Alaska (Rogers, 1986: 207). Mature boreal forest stands reveal a slow down or deterioration as the system reaches maturity in terms of reproduction, plant growth, energy flows and biogeochemical cycles (Feit, 1969: 63). Food resources are unevenly distributed in the Boreal Forest, both spatially and temporally (Rogers, 1986: 206-207), certain species being geographically restricted, often at specific times of the year.

4.1.4 Adaptations to the Boreal Forest

Hunter-gatherers in marginal environments (those characterized by low faunal diversity, resource fluctuations and an unstable unpredictable resource base) have four basic buffering mechanisms (Stein Mandryk, 1993: 52). These mechanisms are 1) mobility, 2) diversification, 3) storage and 4) exchange (Stein Mandryk, 1993: 53). Furthermore, control of population size can be used adaptively in marginal environments, through migration of individuals (Steegman, 1983a: 251, Rogers, 1963a: 71). Hunter-gatherers in the boreal forest lived in a cold, wooded environment with winters lasting five or six months (Brown, 1986: 213). The environment had a marked impact on the course of human affairs in the boreal forest (Steegman, 1983b: 4). Aboriginal hunter-gatherers of the Boreal Forest developed a number of contingencies to deal with resource fluctuations (Tanner, 1979: 59). First and foremost was mobility. Their summer movements were conditioned by the network of waterways and their winter travel was by toboggan or snowshoe (Brown, 1986: 213). There is a correlation between fluctuations in the physical environment and seasonal movements of the population (Hallowell, 1992: 43). Stored foods were used, such as frozen or dried game and fish, or in the contact period, purchased foods (Tanner, 1979: 59, Steegman, 1983a: 252). Fishing efforts would be intensified to alleviate resource stress (Tanner, 1979: 59, Steinbring, 1981: 247, Clelland, 1982). Adipose tissue can also help to defend against resource fluctuation, in that it may be stored against possible starvation, although there is no way that this ethnographically recorded response can be verified archaeologically (Steegman, 1983a: 253). Sharing of food as a means of evening out resource variability is ethnographically documented among Subarctic hunter-gatherers (Steegman, 1983a: 253).

Forest fires were selectively used by the Northern Algonquians to force forest regeneration, attracting desired species of animals and birds, as well as fostering desired floral resources (Brown, 1986: 147). Forest fires also had the effect of opening areas for travel and hunting (Brown and Wilson, 1986: 147). After a forest fire, whether natural or deliberate, a period of relative low- to non-productivity would ensue, often accompanied by abandonment of the region (Feit, 1969: 27). Following a forest fire a brief period would ensue when subsistence was uncertain, but still possible, mostly through reliance on fish as a staple food item (Feit 1969: 92).

While some resources in the boreal forest, such as the beaver, are highly predictable, others, such as the moose, are much less predictable in their movements throughout the year (Feit 1973). However, hunters of the boreal forest have a detailed knowledge of the ethology of the moose and can hunt moose at times when they are aggregated in a few locales and are, therefore, much more predictable (Feit, 1973: 120). For example, the use of bogs and wetlands by moose in summer is well known by local hunters in the boreal forest. This knowledge is built into the formulation of the annual cycle, where seasonally available food resources are targeted for use during periods of peak efficiency (Ray, 1974: 168). Ideally the targeted food resources are organized such that at least two resources are available at any given time (Feit, 1973: 120). Spatial organization is an important factor in the exploitation of animals (Craik and Casgrain, 1986: 181). Despite the fact that the boreal forest is a so-called marginal environment, the situation is not desperate for inhabitants of the region, as it offers resources to those who are skilled in its use (Steegman et al., 1983: 318), but tends to support only small, highly dispersed human populations.

4.1.5 Acculturative Change and the Fur Trade

The fur trade, with its base in trade goods, brought changes to Aboriginal material culture, but also affected subsistence patterns, the seasonal round, social organization and demography (McKennan, 1969: 95). The focus of life changed to the formation of semi-permanent villages built around, or in the environs of, the trading post (McKennan, 1969: 95, Martijn and Rogers, 1969: 99). Hunting shifted from being primarily a subsistence activity to being an economic activity (McKennan, 1969: 95, Rogers, 1963a: 72). The fur trade has caused transformations in Aboriginal society through the introduction of new forms of socio-economic organization. Despite these transformations, the basic subsistence patterns remain relatively similar (Bishop, 1981: 254). It is perhaps more realistic to view culture change as voluntary change, in response to specific ecological or environmental changes, rather than an accommodation to European culture (Fisher, 1969: 10).

In order to understand the nature of acculturative change, one must understand three factors: 1) the time of contact, 2) the nature and intensity of contact and 3) the major cultural changes that resulted (McKennan, 1969: 94). Steward (1969: 293) notes that there are three types of change introduced by European contact with Aboriginal populations: 1) modification of environmental resources, 2) introduction of manufactured resources and 3) the creation of social linkages with external institutions. The primary affect of acculturation on social organization in the boreal forest is likely to be changes in population size or structure due to depopulation or immigration (Damas, 1969: 119). Brody (1988) argues that acculturative change in the seasonal round occurred not in the nature or activities, but in the nature of the travel associated with them. The main difference is the introduction of the snowmobile in 1960, which allowed for more efficient travel to and from the summer aggregation community, which became a more or less permanent settlement. So, acculturative change has not caused a change in hunting activity or has it changed the form of the seasonal round, but it has affected the logistics of the seasonal round. This means that activities and activity areas used in contemporary times have a deeper link to the past activities and activity areas than normally assumed.

Much of the debate amongst Algonquianists concerns the "aboriginality" of the land tenure system associated with the hunting group. In fact it is possible to identify three phases to the debate on land tenure of the Northern Algonquian. The "classic" phase was the belief that the land tenure system described in the ethnohistories and ethnographies was aboriginal, pre-dating the arrival of Europeans (Cooper, 1939, Speck, 1915, Rogers, 1986: 203, Tanner, 1986: 20). The "post-classic" view was that the land tenure system arose due to European influence, mainly by way of the fur trade (Bishop, 1970, Rogers, 1986: 203, Tanner, 1986: 21). The "neoclassic" view does not concern itself so much with when hunting territories arose, but focuses more on management, conservation, ownership and trespass of lands that the Northern Algonquians inhabited (Rogers, 1986: 205). Current thought indicates that while individual hunting territories are a post-contact phenomenon, the concept of territoriality amongst the Algonquians is not (Bishop, 1986: 40).

The acculturative effect of European contact may be more complex than the simple adoption of Euro-Canadian culture, but likely it involves many innovations, which are neither strictly Aboriginal nor Euro-Canadian in nature (Rogers, 1962: 2). One must ask the question of how far an ethnographic analogy can be pushed into prehistory – to what extent do modern groups, or those of post-contact times, represent anything about pre-contact groups (Freeman Jr., 1968: 262, Binford, 1968a, Binford, 1968b, Schrire, 1984). Freeman (1968: 265) argues that parallels must not be assumed to exist before it has been demonstrated that they do. This indicates that, while the ethnographic and ethnohistoric data for the Algonkians must be employed carefully, it is still possible to employ ethnographic analogies to pre-contact groups in the boreal forest, so long as this is done conservatively. The way in which cultural data has been incorporated into the modeling process is described in chapter 2.

Valuable data about the settlement systems of pre-contact hunter-gatherers, which can be employed in the creation of predictive models, clearly exists. This data has to be employed carefully, as is also argued in chapter 2, but can play an important role in helping to predict site locations.

Chapter 5 The Dataset

5.0 The Dataset

This chapter reviews the archaeological dataset that will be employed in the analysis from the point of view of the physical environment (*i.e.* the boreal forest), the study area (*i.e.* the Manitoba Model Forest) and the culture-history of the time period of interest.

5.1 The Boreal Forest

The boreal forest is a global ecozone, representing some seven million square kilometers (Marles et al., 2000). This ecozone is dominated by trees from the genera *Pinus, Picea, Larix* and *Abies* (Scott, 1995: 82), all of which are coniferous tree types. Conifers are well suited to the boreal environment, as they have adaptations which allow them to seek out moisture, tolerate near-saturated soils or cope with strongly acidic, low-nutrient soil types (Scott, 1995: 90). These conditions are characteristic of recently deglaciated areas with high humidity, low evaporation, low elevation and prolific wetland areas (Marles et al., 2000). The boreal forest is one of the largest ecozones in Canada and the dominant forest cover in Canada (Scott, 1995: 82). The extent of the boreal forest in Canada is shown in Figure 4. It stretches from the northern Atlantic coast, sweeping across several provinces and ending in the southwestern Northwest Territories and Yukon. The boreal forest is an ecologically vibrant habitat, with populations of plants and animals interacting in a highly dynamic fashion (Winterhalder, 1983: 9). This ecozone is a region of extreme patchiness, where patches are small, dispersed and irregular in outline (Winterhalder, 1983: 32). Within this broad swath of land there is a great deal of complexity, and there have been attempts to subdivide the region into sub-regions (Winterhalder, 1983: 32), such as the Boreal Shield and the Boreal Plain (Marles et al., 2000), although these subdivisions are not clearly defined and terminology is variable. Alternatively, Scott (1995) refers to the ecoregions in the boreal forest as the open lichen woodland, the northern coniferous forest, and the mixed forest (boreal-broadleaf ecotone). The differences in terminology are due to differences in scale of classifications. The uniting factor of the boreal forest, which maintains it as a unified ecozone, is the climate. Based on the criteria identified in various fields, it also tends to be treated as a coherent region by social, physical and natural scientists (Gardner, 1981: 5), likely for the sake of simplicity more than any other reason. This chapter will focus on the characteristics of the Northern Coniferous Forest ecoregion as it best describes the target region. The study area also can be classified as part of the Canadian Shield, which is characterized by bedrock hills and ridges, interspersed with boggy areas (Gardner, 1981: 6). The Canadian Shield is a vast region of rock outcrops, lakes and ancient rock stretching across Canada in a giant U-shaped swath (Gardner, 1981: 6).

The MbMF study region falls into the Northern Coniferous Forest ecoregion. Here, closed spruce (*Picea sp.*) forests characterize the better-drained soils of the region (Scott, 1995: 94). Wetter regions in the ecoregion are dominated by larch, or tamarack, (*Larix larcinia*) and black spruce (*Picea mariana*) (Scott, 1995: 94). Dry, low quality soils are dominated by pine trees (*Pinus sp.*) (Scott, 1995: 94).

The climate of the region is normally described as cold continental, but, in fact, is actually a series of contiguous ecoclimates, supporting coniferous and mixed-wood forests (Scott, 1995: 83). Generally, all of these ecoclimates support the domination of coniferous tree species over broadleaf deciduous or evergreen tree species (Scott, 1995: 83). The difference between a general cold continental climate and that of the Northern Coniferous Forest, is the high moisture conditions, due to low evaporation rates and high soil moisture retention. These generalized moist and cool conditions result in slow decomposition processes (Scott, 1995: 88).

The boreal forest is extremely dynamic in nature, and mechanisms such as frequent forest fires and succession mean that an extremely varied ecosystem prevails (Feit, 1969). In fact, conifers are so well adapted to fire sequences that some researchers have even speculated that they have adapted to forest-fire dynamics (Scott, 1995 676: 91). Although this is a controversial and the supporting data are unclear, forest fire is one of the most important dynamic variables in the region (Scott, 1995: 91).

The majority of the Northern Coniferous Forest region, and particularly the study area, was covered by the last glaciation, the Wisconsinian (Buchner, 1979), which has resulted in the varied physiography.

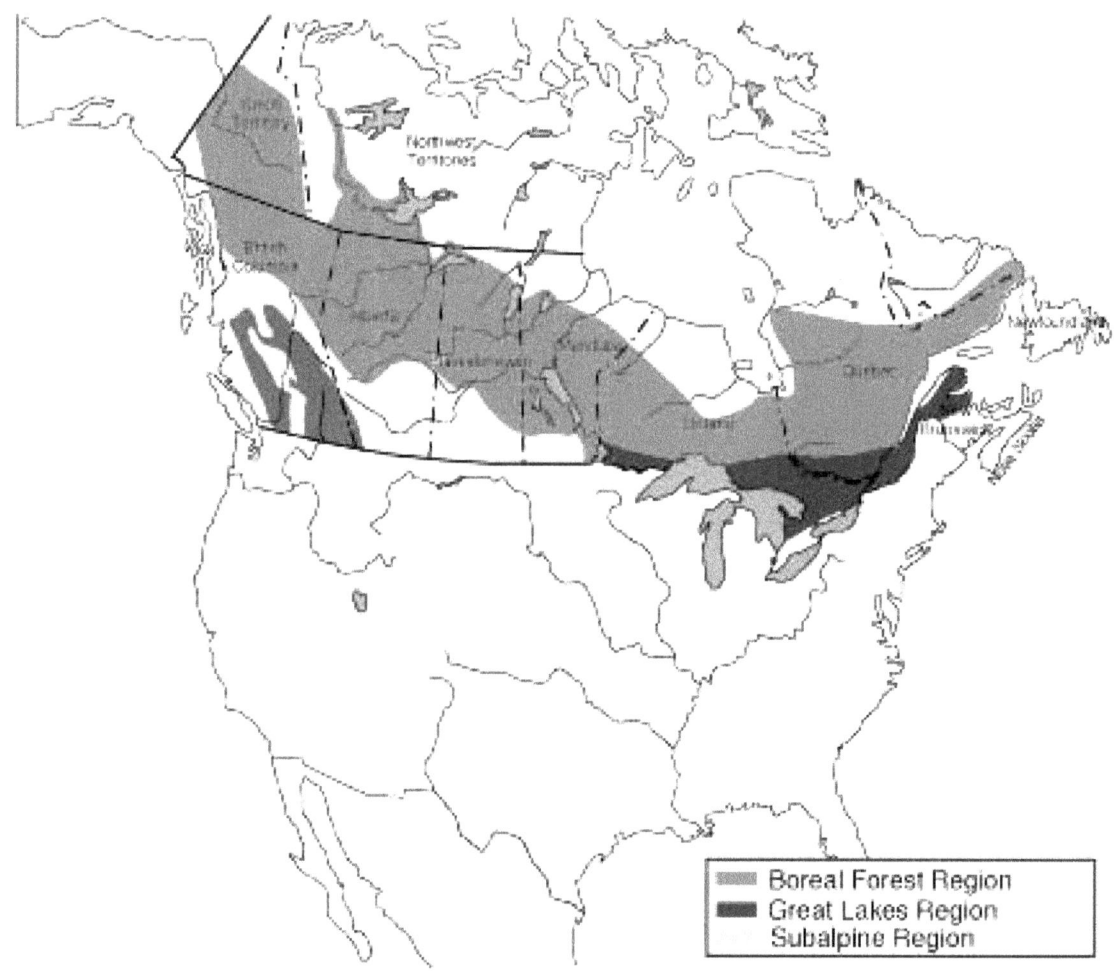

**Figure 4: Boreal Forest Regions of Canada
(Marles et al. 2000)**

Soils in the boreal forest, as a whole, tend to be poorly developed (Gardner, 1981: 6), as pedogenesis is influenced by the climatic conditions, as well as differences in drainage and the parent material (Scott, 1995: 88). Podzols are the dominant soil order of the boreal region (Scott, 1995: 88). They are formed from the regolith of the underlying bedrock under the influence of positive moisture indices, which encourage leaching and acidification (Scott, 1995: 88). Podzols are characterized by strong acidity and low nutrient status (Scott, 1995: 88). Podzols can be recognized by a thick layer of leaf mulch, a leached horizon and a second horizon of organic colloids leached from above (Gardner, 1981: 13).

Many major animal species are found in the boreal forest, including woodland caribou (*Rangifer tarandus caribou*) and moose (*Alces alces*) as the major large mammal species and the major subsistence species of the human inhabitants of the boreal forest (Gillespie, 1981: 15). Other large mammals found in the region, although often with limited distributions, include: black bears (*Ursus americanus*); wood bison (*Bison bison athabascae*); elk (*Cervus elaphus canadensis*); grizzly bears (*Ursus horribilis*); and white-tailed deer (*Odocoileus virginianus*) (Gillespie, 1981: 15). A number of small game resources are also present, such as hare (*Lepus americanus*) and beaver (*Castor canadensis*) (Gillespie, 1981: 15). While there are a variety of fish species available their role in human subsistence is unclear. Gillespie (1981: 15) argues that fish were not considered an important food resource, while other data (e.g. see Malasiuk, 1999, Schwimmer et al., 2002) suggest that fish may have been more important in some pre-contact time periods.

5.1.1 The Manitoba Model Forest

The dataset that will be used in this research comprises some 225,000 hectares of boreal forest, located within the Manitoba Model Forest (MbMF). Forestry companies have become aware of non-timber values of the boreal forest in the past few years (Manitoba Model Forest Inc., 1999: 17), in particular the inherent value of cultural resources. Therefore, the MbMF issued a contract to build an inductive archaeological predictive model of archaeological potential (Contract 99-6-25 to Northern Lights Heritage and L. Larcombe Archaeological Consulting), the MbMF Archaeological Predictive Modeling Project (MbMF APMP), for a study region within the MbMF. Predictive modeling offers a powerful tool to the forestry industry for use in the planning process to protect areas where sites are likely to occur. Initial work on the inductive model for the MbMF study region began in May 1999. The location of the MbMF in Manitoba is shown in Figure 5, and the location of the study are in the MbMF is shown in Figure 6.

The current archaeological database includes over one hundred sites in the study area. The site locations show a littoral bias, as they are predominantly located on the shores of the major lakes, which are generally more developed. The study area has seen little organized archaeological survey or excavation, with the exception of Saylor's (1989) Wanipigow survey and excavations of the 1970's. The majority of the other archaeological sites of the study area are surface scatters, with no diagnostic artifacts, and therefore of an unknown time period. The current archaeological database precludes the modeling of sites by individual cultural period at this time, with the exception of the Middle to Late Woodland Period, which represents the majority of the sites in the study area. Furthermore, modeling by site function is not possible, as site functions are not defined for the majority of sites in the study area.

For several reasons, the research design required that the sites used for the predictive modeling be limited to the late pre-contact period in the study area. First, the potential for extending the land-use data from the community, as discussed in chapter 2, into prehistory was unclear. Concerns about the application of ethnographic data to pre-contact periods have been expressed. Some researchers argue that acculturative change is reflected in the ethnographic record (e.g. McKennan, 1969, Damas, 1969). Conversely, other researchers (e.g. Leacock, 1969, Brody, 1988) do argue that fur trade era patterns described in the ethnographies hold into pre-contact

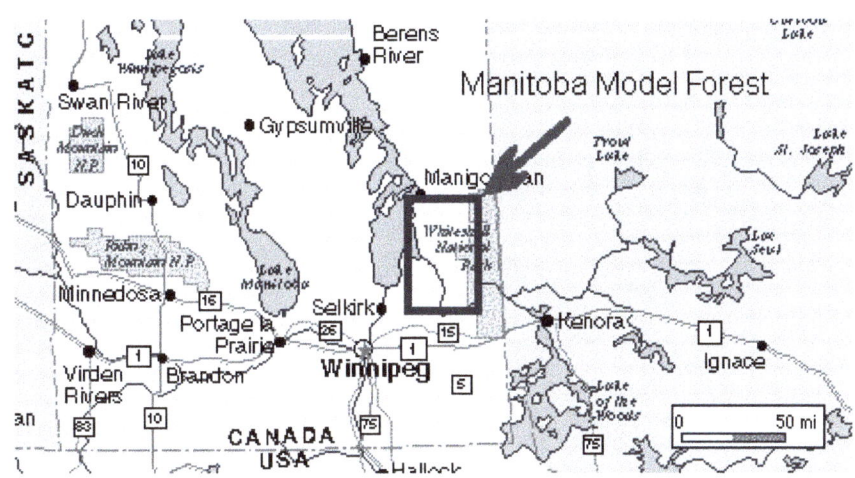

Figure 5: Location of the Manitoba Model Forest

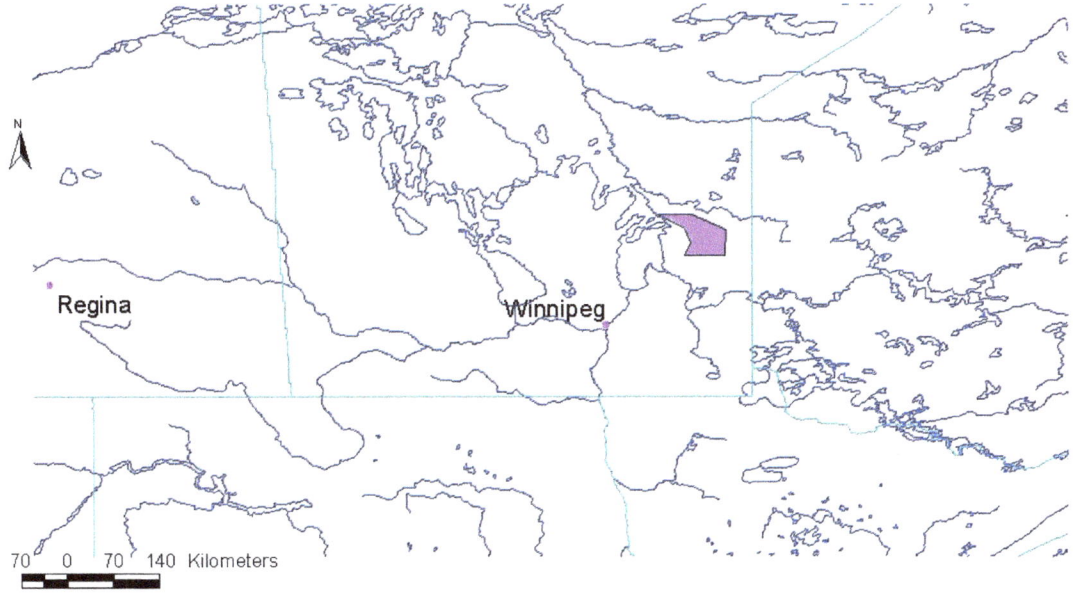

Figure 6: Location of the Study Area

eras, especially at lower levels of social organization, such as the local band. However, this debate remains, for the most part, unresolved. Since it will be used to model the cultural component of the cultural-environmental model, it was decided to limit the application of the cultural data to only the most recent pre-contact (Woodland) period.

Second, the use of economic factors for earlier periods would require detailed paleoenvironmental reconstruction to account for environmental shifts, and corresponding shifts in subsistence. To streamline the research, economic factors are limited to a more recent time frame, when the environmental conditions would have been similar to those observable today. To allow comparison of the two types of model designed for this research, the modeling period is restricted to the Woodland period (ca. 2000 to 300 BP). The list of Woodland sites, their Borden Numbers, and their cultural affiliations are contained in Appendix 1.

Pollen core data from the MbMF region and surrounding areas suggest that from about 3500 BP to the arrival of Europeans in the area, conditions were stable and similar to modern environmental conditions (Petch et al., 2000: 62). Pine (*Pinus*) dominates the pollen samples, and birch (*Betulus*), alder, oak, maple and elm trees are present (Petch et al., 2000: 62).

5.2 Woodland Prehistory of the MbMF Region

The first appearance of pottery is generally considered the watershed event in defining the start of the Middle Woodland period in the target region (Buchner, 1979: 103). The Woodland tradition is thought to originate outside Manitoba and to spread into the area (Schwimmer et al., 2002). However, it is not clear if the spread of Woodland pottery and culture occurred through the movements of populations or the diffusion of the technology. The tradition is named after the eastern woodlands in which it developed and from where it spread (Schwimmer et al., 2002). It is archaeologically visible as four distinct factors: 1) the appearance of ceramics; 2) the creation of burial mounds; 3) adoption of the bow and arrow; and 4) the adoption of horticulture (Schwimmer et al., 2002). While adoption of these four factors was variable throughout North America, all are present in North American Woodland cultures to a greater or lesser degree. Despite the adoption of horticulture elsewhere in the Woodlands cultural area, aboriginal groups in the study area remained heavily dependent on hunting and gathering as a lifestyle (Schwimmer et al., 2002). The Woodland period can be divided into three phases: Laurel, Blackduck and the Western Woodland Algonkian Configuration. These are not strict chronocultures, as demonstrated by their overlapping dates. It is more likely, especially towards the end of the Woodland period, that the phases represent the movement of populations.

5.2.1 The Laurel Phase

The earliest ceramic tradition in the study area during this time period is the Laurel phase (Buchner, 1979: 103), dating from about 1900 BP to about 900 BP (Buchner et al., 1983: 153). Laurel ceramics are conical, grit tempered pots, generally built by coiling (Buchner et al., 1983: 156). Decorations on the pots are either stamped or incised, but the decorations are generally limited to the rim and neck of the pot (Schwimmer et al., 2002). Sites containing Laurel ceramics are widely distributed, in Saskatchewan, Manitoba, Ontario, Quebec, Minnesota and Michigan (Buchner, 1979: 103). Despite this wide distribution, there remains a high degree of homogeneity, both spatially and temporally, in the assemblages found at these sites (Buchner, 1979: 104). Laurel sites hold evidence of a fairly diffuse economic base, including fish and large mammal remains (Buchner, 1979: 107). It has been suggested that the origin of the Laurel culture is quite distant from Manitoba, based on a number of lines of evidence, mostly concerning the sharp discontinuity from the previous archaeological cultures in the region (Buchner, 1979: 111).

Large camps tended to occur in ecotonal boundary areas, such as lakesides, bays and river mouths (Dawson, 1983: 72). These large campsites seem to represent seasonal aggregation sites, and often had satellite camps in close proximity (Dawson, 1983: 73). Due to the acidic soil conditions of the region, faunal preservation tends to be poor, leaving much to speculate about with regards to subsistence activities. However, existing evidence exists points to an elaboration of subsistence patterns from previous time periods, focussed on large mammals (Dawson, 1983: 74) and fishing an important resource (Malasiuk, 1999: 90, Schwimmer et al., 2002). It appears that Laurel people may even have been moving between the boreal forest areas and out into parklands to take advantage of resources such as bison (Meyer and Hamilton, 1994: 110).

5.2.2 The Blackduck Phase

The Laurel Phase in Manitoba is followed by the Blackduck phase (Buchner, 1979: 114), dating from about 1000 BP to 1400 BP (Lenius and Olinyk, 1990). Blackduck does not completely replace Laurel but develops in the south and spreads slowly to the north (Meyer and Hamilton, 1994: 112). Blackduck vessels can be characterized as being large, fragile, globular vessels (Buchner et al., 1983: 128). The vessels tend to be made from local clays and grit tempered (Buchner et al., 1983: 128). Construction of the vessels may have employed textile containers, and pots were decorated with cord-wrapped tool impressions (Buchner et al., 1983: 128) or with a paddle and anvil (Lenius and Olinyk, 1990). This construction technique gives Blackduck vessels a distinctive surface finish, easily recognizable by archaeologists (Lenius and Olinyk, 1990: 79). People of the Blackduck culture eventually spread outside the margins of the boreal forest, moving into the aspen parkland and onto the southern Canadian plains (Buchner et al., 1983: 123-124).

During the Blackduck period, sites tend to be larger and more numerous, suggesting a population increase from the previous Laurel Phase (Dawson, 1983: 77). As in the preceding period, there is a focus on ecotonal boundaries. Sites are situated in the same locations as Laurel Phase sites (Dawson, 1983: 77). Large aggregation sites occur on major lakes and rivers, and smaller sites are located on islands or on minor lakes and rivers (Dawson, 1983: 77).

5.2.3 Western Woodland Algonkian Configuration

The late pre-contact period in the boreal forest is represented by a number of regional wares, the significance of which, in terms of cultural affiliations, is unclear. Lenius and Olinyk (1990) have attempted to organize the archaeological record into two major composites (a grouping of related regional wares) – the Selkirk Composite (Buchner, 1979: 120) and the Rainy River Composite (Lenius and Olinyk, 1990). Many different ceramic wares are classified as part of these composites, such as the Selkirk culture of the Selkirk Composite and the Duck Bay and Sandy Lake cultures of the Rainy River Composite. The main difference between the two composites is the presence or absence of certain design elements from the exterior decoration of the ceramics (Lenius and Olinyk, 1990: 101). The two composites are subsumed into a wider configuration known as the Western Woodland Algonkian Configuration. While not yet fully recognized in the archaeological literature, this appears to be a logical and coherent way to view the complex archaeological record of this time period, and is adopted in this research. These traditions are thought to be outgrowths of the Blackduck and Laurel phases, as the pottery shares many decorative details with ceramic wares from those phases (Lenius and Olinyk, 1990: 101). According to the linguistic evidence, the split between the Cree and Ojibwa languages occurred about 1000 BP (Lenius and Olinyk, 1990: 101), suggesting that the two Late Woodland composites grow out of a ceramic tradition adopted by a proto-Algonkian people (*i.e.* the Laurel and Blackduck phases) who split into Cree and Ojibwa groups. The Cree are argued to be associated with the Selkirk Composite and the Ojibwa with the Rainy River Composite (Lenius and Olinyk, 1990).

Other datasets employed in the modeling process include land-use data, environmental data and economic data. The land-use data, as discussed in chapter 2, contains information about resources available to and employed by local First Nations groups, including data on the location of vegetative, faunal and other natural resources. The environmental dataset includes data on the slope, aspect, distance to lakes and rivers and tree types, and is discussed in chapter 6. The economic dataset is based on habitat suitability indices for moose and woodland caribou, and is also discussed in chapter 6. The models created in this research are founded on the analysis of these datasets in relation to the archaeological dataset.

Chapter 6 Methodology

6.0 Methodology

This research involves the creation of four models. This chapter discusses the methods used to create the models. Of the four models, three use the same methodology on different sets of variables and two use identical variable sets but different methods, namely logistic regression (a weighted value method) and the CARP methodology (a weighted intersection method) (Dalla Bona, 1994b, Dalla Bona, 1994a). These two methodologies will be discussed separately below. This chapter also will examine the field methods employed to test the models and how the models will be evaluated.

6.1 Data Collection

Much of the data have come from the MbMF and project partners, who have provided data in digital format for many environmental variables, including: 1) an elevation survey (air photo survey, sampled at intervals of 250m with higher density samples in the littoral zone); 2) the Forest Resource Inventory (1987 and 1997); 3) land use data collected from a previous project for the MbMF in point format (Petch and Larcombe, 1998); and 4) a set of orthographically rectified aerial photographs of the study region.

Additional data was digitized as required, such as hydrologic data and the location of islands. Digitizing was done using the computer facilities of the Anthropology Lab, University of Manitoba. The lab currently features a Pentium Celeron 333 MhZ computer with 128 MB of RAM and an 8 MB Video Card. Capture of data was achieved through the use of a Calcomp DrawingBoard III large format digitizer. This digitizer is 24x36 inches with .254 mm accuracy (400 lpmm accuracy). Digitizing was done through the digitizing functions of the Arcview 3.2 software. The datasets employed in the modeling are shown in Appendix 2.

6.2 Statistical Testing of the Variables

All of the variables employed in the each of the models were tested for statistical significance. The method for testing the variables follows the procedure set out in Kvamme (1990), as discussed in Chapter 2. Results of the Kolmogorov-Smirnov test for each of the variables are included in Appendix 2. The details of the testing procedure are discussed below.

Some terminology must be explained here, where the software employed (ArcView) differs from normal usage of terms in GIS. For the purposes of this research, the ArcView terminology is adopted over the conventional terminology. ArcView uses the terminology "theme" to refer to what is normally called a "data layer" ((Burrough, 1986). Additionally, shape files are an approximation in ArcView of the vector data format, and grid files are an approximation of the raster data format (Burrough 1986).

The first step in the statistical testing is to analyze the known site locations against the environmental, cultural or economic variables in order to determine significance of each the variables employed. To accomplish this, the site theme is first selected as the active theme in ArcView 3.2 GIS and then *Summarize Zones* from the *Analysis* Menu is chosen. This procedure lists the values of a particular environmental variable for all of the sites in the archaeological database. The field containing the Borden number of the sites is chosen as the field that describes the data. The resultant table then has the environmental variable of interest for each of the sites individually. ArcView creates a table with the site Borden Number, and the value(s) for the environmental variable at that location. Since the site theme is a point theme and the Borden Number is a unique identifier for the site, the minimum and maximum values for the environmental variable are the same. The *XTools* menu command *Export to Excel Spreadsheet* is selected to send the table data to an Excel spreadsheet. In Excel, the field containing the Borden numbers of the sites and the *Max* field are chosen as the fields to be imported. The remainder of the analysis then takes place in Excel. First, the sites are organized into classes. For example, if one were looking at slope and sites, each of the sites would be assigned to one of the slope classes of interest (*i.e.* 0, 0-5, 5-10, 10-15 and 15+). The numbers of sites falling into each category is then tabulated and the cumulative percentage of sites falling into each category is calculated. The number of cells in the environment is calculated through the use of the Map Calculator, by writing queries that return the number of cells that are true for the expression entered. For example, to calculate the slope classes, expressions are written to return the number of cells where slope is equal to zero, where slope is greater than zero and less than or equal to five, and so forth. The number of cells in each class for the background environment is also converted to a cumulative percent. The difference between the cumulative percentages of cells in the environment and the cumulative percent of sites for each class is then calculated. The absolute value of that difference is the value of interest. This maximum difference is then compared against the critical value, as described in Kvamme (1990) and outlined in chapter 2. If the maximum difference exceeds the critical value, then the result is said to be statistically significant and the alternative hypothesis is accepted. If the maximum difference does not exceed the critical value, then there is no statistical significance and the null hypothesis is accepted. With eighty-one Woodland sites in the study area, the critical value is 0.151, at the 0.05 level of significance.

6.3 Preparation of Data for All Models

The initial step in predictive modeling is to prepare all of the themes required for the analysis. Each type of variable (*i.e.* environmental, cultural and economic) is prepared differently, as discussed below.

6.3.1 Environmental Variable Preparation

For each of the environmental variables two steps are required before analysis can begin. First, the themes must be generated from the raw data. This may also include secondary data products like the slope and aspect themes (Burrough, 1986). Second, these themes need to be prepared before they can be employed in the model. The following discussion explains the steps that were taken to generate and prepare each of the variables.

The elevation data provided for this study is in the form of a database of three-dimensional points. The points cover the northing, easting and elevation. From this elevation data, a digital elevation model (DEM) is created in ArcView 3-D Analyst through the *Surface* menu, choosing the *Create TIN from features* option. The DEM itself is primarily used to derive the slope and aspect themes, both of which are also done from selections from the *Surface* menu. The *Surface* menu offers selections to *Derive Slope* and *Derive Aspect*. It is with these menu commands that the slope and aspect themes are created. Water buffers are created around lakes and rivers individually through the use of the *Theme* menu's *Create Buffers* command. The parameters set in the ensuing dialogue boxes have five 100-meter buffers. Additional parameters of the buffers may be selected in the ensuing dialogue boxes. River and lake buffers are selected to be only external to the features (*i.e.* to calculate the distance away from the lakes/rivers, not into them), dissolving overlapping buffers. Once these themes are created or imported into ArcView, the data can be prepared.

Many of the generated themes are in ArcView shape format. The Map Calculator in ArcView cannot work with shape files, but can only be used on grid files. Therefore all shape files must be converted to the appropriate format. Some grid files, like the derived slope and aspect themes, do not have associated tables, which are needed for adding the weighted values used in the CARP-style cultural-environmental model. In order to give themes, specifically the slope and aspect themes, a table the Map Calculator is used to make a calculated grid theme. The Map Calculator queries the theme in question to identify areas matching the desired parameters. For example, in the case of the slope theme, the Map Calculator queries the theme for each of the individual slope categories (*i.e.* slope = 0, slope > 0 and slope <=5, etc.). The Map Calculator gives a result of 1 for those areas that match the criteria in question and a result of 0 for those areas that do not match. In order to add these individual classes together to create the grid files for the CARP method model, it is necessary to add an additional field to the table, giving each query a unique number.

Each query returns a result of "1" for those areas that match the query criteria. Therefore, adding the results of separate queries would just result in a score of "1" across the entire study area. Therefore, it is necessary to add a class value to each of the query's results to differentiate one area from another. An example of this is shown in Figure 7. In the case of slope, a field is added to each of the calculations' table, which is given an arbitrary value (*e.g.* slope of 0 = 1, slope of 0-5 degrees =2, slope of 5-10 degrees =3, etc.). This allows each of the calculations to be combined into a single grid theme. This grid theme will have the arbitrary class values assigned to it, but the legend can be changed to represent the underlying meaning of the class values. A combined theme as described is illustrated in Figure 7. In Figure 8 the *Value* field is the arbitrary value assigned to the calculation. It is this value that is added to get the calculated grid theme for slope and aspect. This step is only necessary for the CARP-style model. For the logistic regression models, the slope and aspect themes, as calculated by 3-D Analyst, suffice to do the calculation. This is a potential advantage of the logistic regression method, in that continuous values of the data can be employed, as opposed to discrete classes, which may hide some of the variation in the data (Menard, 1995). Additionally, since logistic-regression does not require the addition of the values to tables, preparation time for logistic regression models is lower.

Another consideration when converting files to grid files is whether or not the coverage of the theme matches the study area. When ArcView's Map Calculator adds grid themes together, it only does so where all the themes intersect. Therefore, themes such as the distance to water buffers (which do not cover the entire study area) must be manipulated into covering the entire study area. This can be done one of two ways. For either approach, it is necessary to create a polygon theme representing the study area. This polygon will be used to extend the coverage of incomplete themes.

The first method of completing this task is more complex. Using the XTools extension, the *Erase* menu option is selected. The study area theme is the polygon from which features are erased; the incomplete shape file is selected as the erasing theme. Once an erase theme is created, the Geoprocessing Wizard extension, found in the *View* menu, is selected to merge the themes to create a single theme from the erase theme and the incomplete theme. This results in a theme with complete coverage for the study area.

A second simpler approach is also found in the Geoprocessing Wizard. The *Union Themes* option is selected, ensuring that the fields are preserved from the incomplete theme, and not from the study area theme. The resultant polygon theme has complete coverage of the study area. Both of these methods were tested during the preparation of the grid themes, and the second was adopted as the method of choice, as it required considerably less computing time.

Finally, all the themes are converted to grid themes, if they are not already grid themes (*e.g.* the slope and aspect themes) using the *Theme* menu's *Convert to Grid* option. Once all of these steps are completed, the data is ready to be manipulated either for the CARP cultural/environmental model or the logistic regression models.

6.3.2 Economic Model Variable Preparation

The moose and caribou model were derived from a wildlife biology study done for the MbMF (Palidwor et al., 1995, Palidwor and Schindler, 1995). These models consider the types of habitat desirable for moose and for woodland caribou. Factors considered in the creation of the Habitat Suitability Index (HSI) for moose and caribou included age of tree stands, crown closure (also referred to as canopy density) and dominant species. For moose, separate winter and summer HSI models are created, reflecting the different habitats that moose tend to prefer in winter and summer seasons. An overall moose HSI value is calculated by averaging the winter and summer HSI values (Palidwor et al., 1995). The models are designed to make HSI calculations based on the 1987 Forest Resource Inventory (FRI). Although a newer FRI has recently been released, the data collected does not contain the same fields as the 1987 FRI, as required for the HSI calculations. The formulae provided to calculate these variables required specific fields to be employed in the HSI calculations. Since some of the data collected used different class values, it was not possible to use the 1997 inventory to do the HSI calculations, as the variable weightings could not be transferred to the new data values collected.

The moose HSI is calculated using three equations: a summer HSI, a winter HSI and an overall HSI.

The Summer HSI is calculated through the combination of calculations for summer food and summer cover. Summer food is calculated by weighting stand type composition, successional stage and crown closure class (Palidwor et al., 1995).

Summer cover is calculated by weighting values of stand type composition, successional stage and crown closure class (Palidwor et al., 1995).

While these appear to be the same calculation the factors are weighted differently in terms of their effect on the variables. The variable weights reflect their importance for either food value or cover value respectively. What Palidwor *et al* (1995) provide is the specific weightings for the variables involved. The actual calculation of the HSI values was done in the course of this research.

Similarly, the winter HSI is calculated by combinations of winter food and winter cover (Palidwor et al., 1995): The winter food is also calculated by weighting stand cover type composition, successional stage and crown closure class. Winter cover calculations are based on the same factors as the summer calculation, but the variables are given different weightings, depending on their winter or summer food values or cover values. The overall moose HSI is then calculated by averaging the summer and winter HSI scores.

The values of the HSI for summer, winter and overall are scaled from zero to one. Scores of zero for HSI are completely unsuitable, and scores of one are highly suitable. The study area moose HSI had relatively low HSI scores, as many of the desired food species for moose were not present. The maximum score obtained in the study area was an overall HSI of 0.65.

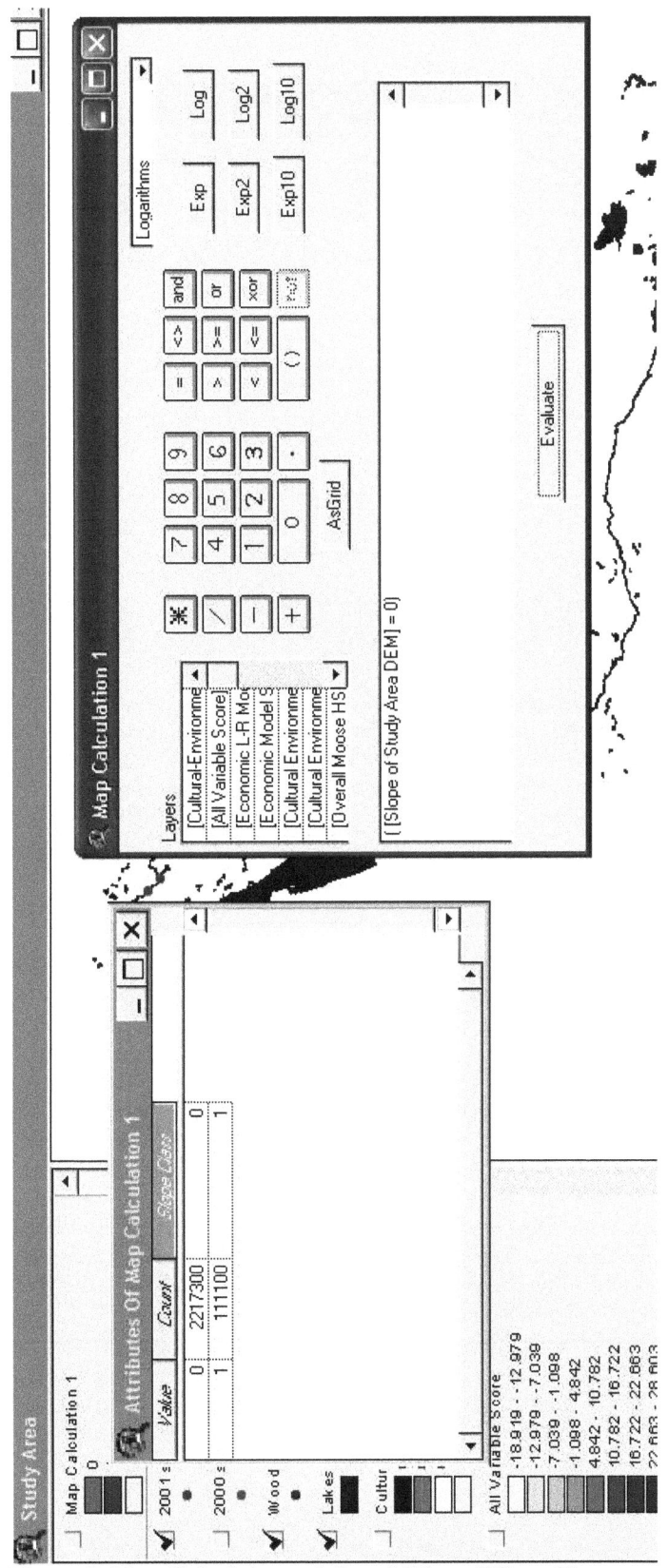

Figure 7: Map Calculator and the addition of Slope Classes

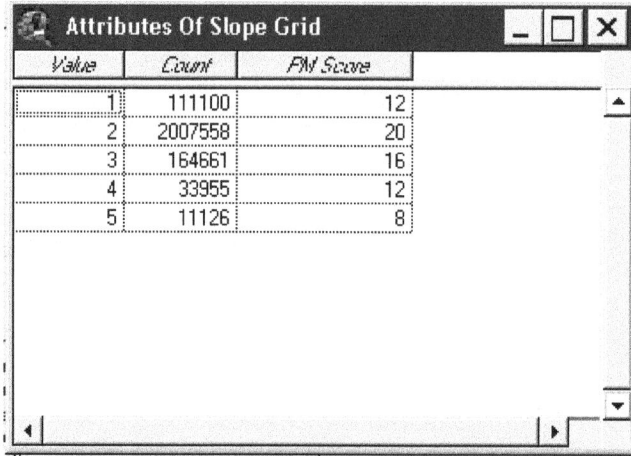

Figure 8: Class Values in a Calculated Grid

The woodland caribou HSI is calculated in a similar manner, but creates a single year-round HSI score for caribou habitat (Palidwor and Schindler, 1995). The equation uses four variables to make the calculation. The caribou HSI is calculated by weighting aspects of species, cutting class, moisture and canopy density (Palidwor and Schindler, 1995).

The study area contained a number of highly suitable habitats for woodland caribou, with a significant amount of the study area receiving a HSI of 1 (high suitability for woodland caribou habitat).

6.4 The CARP Cultural/Environmental Model Construction

The methodology for the CARP cultural/ environmental model was derived from the information contained in the CARP publications (Dalla Bona, 1994a, Dalla Bona, 1994b). However, some aspects of the modeling process are poorly explained in these publications. Some interpolation had to be done in order to complete the model itself, particularly the way in which the variables were weighted. The description of the weighting process was not clearly conveyed in the study and had to be constructed for this research.

6.4.1 Methodology for Environmental Model

Some of the discrete classes of variables were created for the CARP methodology using non-arbitrary classes, while others were divided into arbitrary classes. The aspect map had obvious classes, the directions of the compass, into which it could be divided. However, variables like distance to water did not have the same obvious divisions. Therefore, the same discrete classes used in the CARP methodology were adopted.

In the CARP methodology, two types of weight are assigned. A weight for a class of variables, referred to as a "class weight", which is assigned to the variable as a whole. The discrete values that variables can take are also assigned a weight, referred to as a "spot weight".

The weighting of maps is done by multiplying the class weight by the spot weight, assigning the resultant that value to each cell in the theme. This is also shown in Figure 6-2, where the ranks for the slope theme are shown in the field *PM Score*. Slope received a class score of 4. Spot scores were assigned according to the discrete values that slope could take (*i.e.* slope=0, slope = 0-5, slope = 5-10, slope =10-15, slope =15+). The field of PM Score then represents the score given to each cell of the theme based on its discrete value.

Class weights are assigned based on the objective data given in the statistical testing. Class scores are determined based on the magnitude of the D_{max} value. The environmental variable with the highest D_{max} value receives the highest class score. Lower D_{max} values are assigned progressively lower class scores. Spot weights tended to be based both on those objective testing data and some subjective assumptions made by the archaeologist. For the spot weights, the weighting is primarily done by examining the distribution of sites within the class. For example, the slope class with the most sites receives the highest spot weight. Other classes receive weights in relation to the number of sites they have in that class. For example, with the aspect variables, those aspect classes which had the most sites in the class were given the highest spot scores. Descending scores were given to lower numbers of site in each of the other classes. However, for some variables subjective criteria were used to establish spot weights. For example, the vast majority of sites fell within the 100 meter distance to lakes buffer and either no sites or few sites fell in the 200, 300, 400, 500 and 500+ distance to lakes buffers. Therefore, a subjective decision was made to give spot scores to each of the buffer distances, decreasing as the distance from water sources grew greater, both on common sense grounds, as well as *a priori* ethnographic knowledge that sites were located inland short distances from lakes. The class and spot weights for each of the environmental variables are shown in Appendix 4.

The product of the class and spot weight values for each environmental variable is then transferred back to the

ArcView table for each grid theme, and entered in a field dedicated to the predictive model score, as illustrated in Figure 6-2. Once each of the environmental grid themes has been weighted, the creation of the environmental model is done through the addition of each of the weighted grid themes using the Map Calculator. The resultant calculated theme is then divided into three equal intervals which are re-labelled as high, medium and low potential in the legend.

6.4.2 Methodology for Cultural Model

The classes of cultural data used in this research are discussed in chapter 2. The data received from the Manitoba Model Forest was a single point theme containing points for all of the land-use data types together. Each of these categories is divided into its own grid theme. This is done by using a simple extension downloaded from the ESRI website, called AddXY. This extension determines the X and Y coordinates of each data point and writes the coordinates to the table of the theme. Each of the classes of land-use data is put into a separate spreadsheet in Excel and saved as a DBF format file. The tables are then added to ArcView in the Tables section. In the project view, from the *View* menu, the *Add Event Theme* option is selected to add the land-use information to the ArcView project.

Buffers are created around each point of land-use data individually through the use of the *Theme* menu's *Create Buffers* command. The parameters set in the ensuing dialogue boxes have one 3000 meter buffer created with non-dissolution of overlapping buffers. Land use data must have complete study area coverage in order to be used in the Map Calculator (as was the case for distance to lakes and rivers buffers). This task is accomplished in the same manner as the environmental data, as described above.

Each of the buffers must be weighted at this time. The weightings are done based on a number of considerations, as explained in chapter 2 of this dissertation. The table for the land use data theme has a field added to it, into which the weights are added for each of the 3000 meter buffers.

The land-use themes, which are now extended to match the entire study area, are converted to grid themes using the *Theme* menu's *Convert to Grid* option. The field selected for the grid theme's value is the field containing the predictive modeling weights.

The cultural model is created by adding the value of the weighted buffers together for each of the classes of land use data together in the Map Calculator.

6.4.3 Methodology for the Combined Model

The creation of a combined environmental-cultural model is a matter of adding together the cultural and the environmental models using the Map Calculator. The resultant theme's range of values is then separated into three equal categories, which are re-labeled high, medium and low potential in the legend.

6.5 Logistic Regression Models

The same procedure is followed for the creation of the cultural/environmental model, the economic model and the cultural/environmental/ economic model. All of these models are created using logistic regression.

The first step is to gather data for all of the variables of interest in an Excel spreadsheet. This is done in a similar fashion to the CARP model procedures, but the data were collected into an individual spreadsheet. The reason for this difference between the CARP methodology and the logistic regression methodology is the CARP methodology considers each of the variables individually, where the logistic regression equation is solved by weighting the influence of all the variables in the analysis simultaneously. Each site has a value for each environmental, cultural or economic variable. An additional field was added to the spreadsheet, called the response variable. The response variable is the result of what is being predicted. In the case of this research the response is a site location. The response variable is used by the statistical software as the prediction by the logistic regression equation. For each site, the response variable "site" was entered. In order to do logistic regression, non-site data is necessary in order to analyze both a positive responses to the predictor variables, as well as negative responses to the predictor variables. In order to create non-site locations a random point generator script downloaded for ArcView. This script was used to generate one hundred random points for the study area polygon. A number of the random points were discarded, as they fell into lakes or coincided with sites. A final total of eighty-nine random non-site points were available for use in the logistic regression equation, the location of which is shown in Figure 9. Non-site data was collected during the field work phases of the research, it was not used in the logistic regression modeling because the sampling locations of this data were in discrete areas that were adjacent to many sites and did not have good coverage through many different ecotones. The non-site data collected was very similar to where the sites were found. Non-site sample locations also lay within 50 meters of site sample locations. Therefore, it was decided that this could create problems in the discrimination of site and non-site locations. Random points offered an alternative to field collected data. Random points could be located away from sites and across all of the microenvironments in the study area. The danger of using a random point generator in areas that have not been surveyed is the possibility, however small, that the random point generated could be a site. The apparent benefits of employing randomly generated points

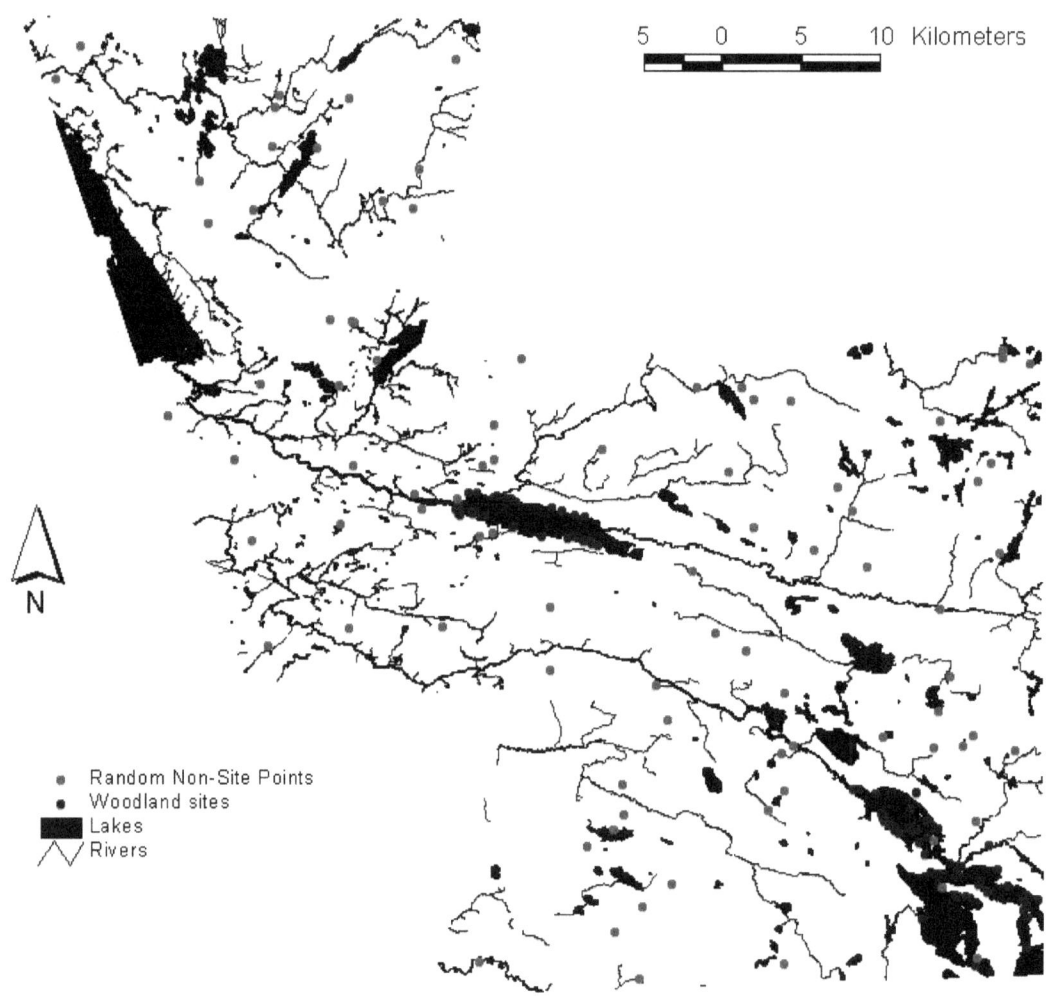

Figure 9: Random Point Locations

as non-sites, in the context of this research, outweighs the small probability that one of the random points might be a site. The number of random points generated was limited in order to limit the probability of generating a non-site, which is in reality a site. The greater the number of random points generated for non-site points, the greater the risk that one may actually be a site.

Environmental, cultural and economic variables values are determined for each of the random points. The site and non-site data are entered into a master spreadsheet, and the spreadsheet is transferred to SPSS for the completion of the logistic regression equation. The logistic regression equation is calculated as follows:

$$y = \beta_0 + \beta_1 x_1 + \ldots + \beta_n x_n + \varepsilon$$

where y is the response variable being predicted, β_0 is the intercept value, and $\beta_n x_n$ are the modifiers (β) and the variables (x). This is done for "n" number of variables (Menard, 1995). Logistic regression works in much the same way as of simple regression, where an independent (or predictor) variable is used to predict the dependent (or response) variable. The advantage of logistic regression over simple regression is that logistic regression can be done with multiple independent variables (Menard, 1995).

Once the logistic regression equation is solved for all of the variables, the equation is returned to ArcView for the creation of the archaeological potential maps. This is achieved through the use of the Map Calculator. In the Map Calculator, each of the environmental, cultural or economic variables is multiplied by the modifier determined through the logistic regression equation.

6.6 Evaluation of Models

Model testing can occur in two forums – the lab and the field. Validation can be done through the assessment of model accuracy based on internal criteria or on a portion of the target sample, which is withheld from the model building process (Kohler and Parker, 1986: 430). In the case of this research, the primary method for evaluating the predictive power of the model is through the use of field testing.

As discussed below, some of the new sites discovered on survey had to be eliminated from the models. From the 2000 survey, four sites had to be removed as they had only historic period components. From the 2001 survey, seven sites were removed as they fell outside the study area and a further two sites were removed as they only had a historic period component. Twenty-eight new sites will be used to evaluate the model predictions.

The highest level of accuracy in APM is gained through models based on data collected during probability-based surveys (BRW Inc., 1996). Therefore, the importance of field-testing of the models is paramount. Field-testing occurred in the study area in the summers of 2000 and 2001. The field testing was based not only on the results from the initial cultural-environmental model created using the CARP method for the MbMF, but it was also designed as a stratified random survey encompassing many types of local environment. By doing the survey in this manner, it expands the knowledge of the land use patterns of pre-contact hunter-gatherers in this region. The importance of stratified testing in all environments and levels of archaeological potential cannot be overstated. If any biases exist in the database of known archaeological site locations, those biases will be carried over into the model (Kvamme, 1988b). Therefore, testing must be carried out even in areas that are not indicated as suitable for habitation by the current archaeological record.

Models are evaluated in chapter 8 using three methods. First, a survey statistic is used that calculates the percentage of the total study area that would have to be surveyed using each method (*i.e.* the total percentage of cells in high and medium potential) and what percentage of sites will be found on that survey. This ratio is determined for: 1) the sites used in the creation of the models; and 2) the sites found during the 2000 and 2001 surveys.

The second method of testing the predictive power of the models is to use random non-site points to compare the predictions. The predictive model values for the new (survey) sites and for the non-sites are compared using the Kolmogorov-Smirnov test, as discussed in chapter 2, to compare the prediction values of sites and non-sites. The critical value, based on 28 new sites being compared to the eighty-nine randomly generated non-site points is 0.2570, at the 0.05 level of significance. For there to be a significant result, the D_{max} value will have to exceed 0.2570.

The final evaluation method is the gain statistic (Kvamme, 1988a). The gain statistic is calculated by:

$$Gain = 1 - \left(\frac{percentage\ of\ total\ area\ in\ PM}{percentage\ of\ total\ sites\ within\ PM\ area} \right)$$

The gain statistic calculates the "gain" for the combined areas of high and medium archaeological potential for each model. Gain is scaled from zero to one, with a gain of one representing high predictive power, and a gain of zero representing low predictive power. The gain statistic is calculated for: 1) sites used in the predictive model creation; and 2) new sites discovered on survey.

6.6.1 Field Methods – Summer 2000

The Summer 2000 project was primarily designed to test two main questions. First, it was apparent that the locations of sites in the study area had a marked littoral bias. The majority of sites were located on the shores of major lakes. It was unclear if this was an archaeological bias or a cultural pattern in the study area. Certainly, the ethnographic record suggests that for boreal forest groups, the shores of the major lakes were the focus of summer encampments (e.g. Larcombe, 1994, Malasiuk, 1999). The ethnographic record also suggests that smaller lakes or inland areas were the focus of smaller groups during winter months. Therefore, part of the summer 2000 field program was designed to test the ethnographic information. The survey was also designed to test areas of high, medium and low archaeological potential for sites, as defined by the first cultural-environmental CARP method model created for the MbMF.

A field crew of nine aboriginal high school students from the community of Hollow Water was hired, supervised by three graduate students from the University of Manitoba. From this group three field crews were formed, each composed of three high school students and a graduate student supervisor. The Wanipigow River, Round Lake, Horseshoe Lake and Rice Lake, as shown in Figure 10, were identified as targeted areas for investigation for a variety of reasons. First, there were no known archaeological sites in these areas. Second, there was a good mix of the three classes of archaeological potential in the region. Third, the lakes were smaller than many of the lakes in the region, but still connected to the main lakes (*i.e.* the Wanipigow and Manicotagan lake systems) where most of the known archaeological sites in the area are located. This would mean that travel to and from these lakes would have been possible through the river network. Finally, these lakes represented a variety of microenvironments that could be explored for sites. The general field methodology followed throughout the summer was to start at the lake or river shore and walk transects outward from the shore, testing at regular intervals. Initially these transects were designed to be one kilometer long, based on double the water buffer distance. Each of the small lakes received minimally one transect in each cardinal direction out form the shore and a return transect parallel and approximately 50 meters apart. On Rice Lake additional transects were done in each cardinal direction. Some transects were shorter, due to difficult local environmental conditions (*e.g.* cliff faces that could not be safely descended or ascended) and the extremely wet and boggy conditions encountered in summer 2000. On the transects, a line of test pits was dug at approximately 100 meter intervals, based on GPS readings. However, as the field season progressed, it was decided to sample the first one hundred meters at 10 meter intervals, as sites seemed to occur only in the first 100 meters away from the lakes. After the first hundred meters, the transects were sampled at 100 meter intervals. Test pits were 25x25 centimeters in area and dug by trowel until either lacustrine clay deposits or bedrock was encountered. Due to the depressed rate of pedogenesis in the region, the completion of test pits was often accomplished by flipping over the moss layer to check the root mat for artifacts.

At each test pit location, the crew completed survey data forms. The location of the test pits, determined by GPS and the UTM coordinates, were recorded on the survey data forms. Data recorded on the survey forms included aspects of the physical environment, such as slope, aspect and distance to water (when it could be determined), as well as aspects of the natural environment such as the tree types present and ground vegetation. The soil strata were also recorded and any finds that were collected. Survey data forms were completed for all test pit locations. A total of 590 test locations were recorded, with over 2000 test pits dug during the four week field season. Twenty-one new archaeological sites were discovered during the survey. At each of these sites, additional test pits were dug to determine the nature and extent of the site when possible. These sites and their Borden Numbers, as well as their relative age, are listed in Appendix 1. Of these, 14 are located in zones of medium archaeological potential, 2 are recorded in zones of high potential and the remaining 5 were found in zones of low archaeological potential, based on the first generation cultural-environmental CARP method model created for the MbMF. Of these sites, four are historic period sites and are not used in the evaluation of the models. Three types of site were found in the survey: historic sites, lithic procurement sites and lithic scatters.

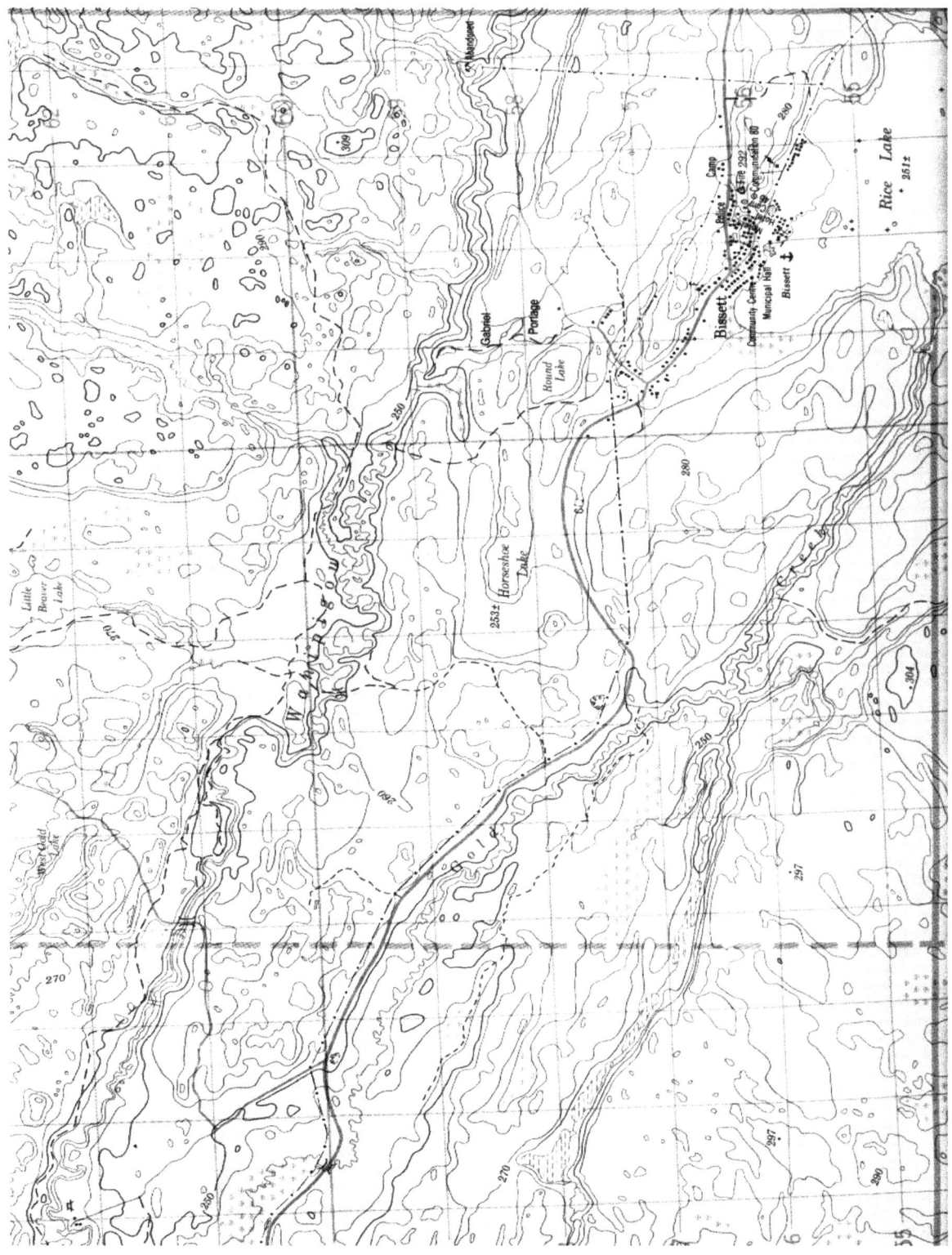

**Figure 10: The Summer 2000 Study Area
(National Topographic Series 1:50000 Map)**

The ephemeral nature of many of the sites found on these smaller lakes suggests that the sites were occupied only on a short-term basis. The lithic scatter sites tended to be small, with very low artifact densities. These sites generally had no diagnostic artifacts and no organic preservation. The low artifact densities can be taken as confirmation that the smaller lakes were used in pre-contact periods by small groups, probably as wintering locations (based on the ethnographic information), especially when contrasted with the high density sites of the major lake margins.

The field season of the summer of 2000 achieved its goals. It examined whether the littoral bias in the data was real or apparent. The field crews worked in extremely difficult environments to test the hinterlands (away from the lakes) for sites. None of the new sites were located any further from these smaller lakes than sites located near larger lakes. Given the terrain and the resources available away from the lakeshore, it is perhaps not surprising that almost nothing was found in the way of archaeological sites in these areas. The cultural-environmental model was validated as being able to predict sites, based on the locations of new sites and their potential from the initial model created using the CARP methodology. However, several lessons were learned from the summer's fieldwork. First, the importance of cultural variables was confirmed. The five sites located in low potential areas were lithic procurement or potential ceremonial sites. These sites would have been used for reasons linked to the presence of factors not considered in a traditional environmental model. Second, the lack of cartographic precision of the known archaeological database was confirmed. During the last week of the survey, some of the sites on the large lakes, specifically Wanipigow Lake, were visited and some testing was done at those sites. Most of the existing site coordinates recorded in the 1970's and 1980's were estimated positions on topographic maps.

The data collected from the 2000 field season were used to modify subsequent model design through the strengthening of the cultural variables and re-examination of the existing site database to fix positional errors.

6.6.2 Field Methods – Summer 2001
The second field season was designed to fulfill different functions in terms of this research. The first field season confirmed that predictive modeling would work and suggested the importance of the cultural data. The second season was designed to test other aspects of the models, notably the testing of the cultural data. First, an Elder from the Hollow Water community was enlisted to help the field crews in order to test cultural land-use data available for the area. The community of Hollow Water selected the Elder. The gentleman is a trapper who has trapped extensively in the study area. The Elder spent six days on the Rice River and Shallow Lake, as shown in Figure 11, directing the field crews to areas that had been used traditionally by the community. Excavations were done at these locations. Rice River and Shallow Lake were chosen because they were important to the community through time and there were no known archaeological sites on either system. However both systems were known to be used by members of the community of Hollow Water. The Hollow Water community was actually originally located on the mouth of Rice River before relocating to its current location. Second, a number of forestry cut block areas were selected in the Beaver Creek region (see Figure 12) for archaeological survey and testing, to look at additional areas away from major lakes to re-confirm that the littoral pattern in the archaeological database was real and not artificial. Cut blocks were chosen, because it was hoped that archaeological visibility would be improved as a result of the forestry activities.

Eight of the nine high school students employed in 2000 were re-employed by the project in 2001. A replacement crew member was hired to replace the student who was no longer available. The Elder directed the field crew during the Rice River survey phase, identifying places where he knew that the "old people" (the past two or three generations) hunted, gathered plants or camped. The crew surveyed and tested at these locations. Portages were also a focus of the field survey, because these are ethnographically known to be focal points for the peoples of the boreal forest (e.g. Malasiuk, 1999, Larcombe, 1994). Field survey forms were completed in the summer 2001 survey for each location tested. The forms were modified slightly, based on information collected in 2000, as is shown in Appendix 6. All tree types around the test locations and the dominant tree type in the immediate vicinity of the testing location was identified. The field survey lasted ten days and identified twenty-two new sites, many of them stratified multi-component sites with diagnostic artifacts. The list of these sites and their cultural affiliations is shown in Appendix 1. Eighteen of the sites are classified as either Woodland or Late Pre-Contact.

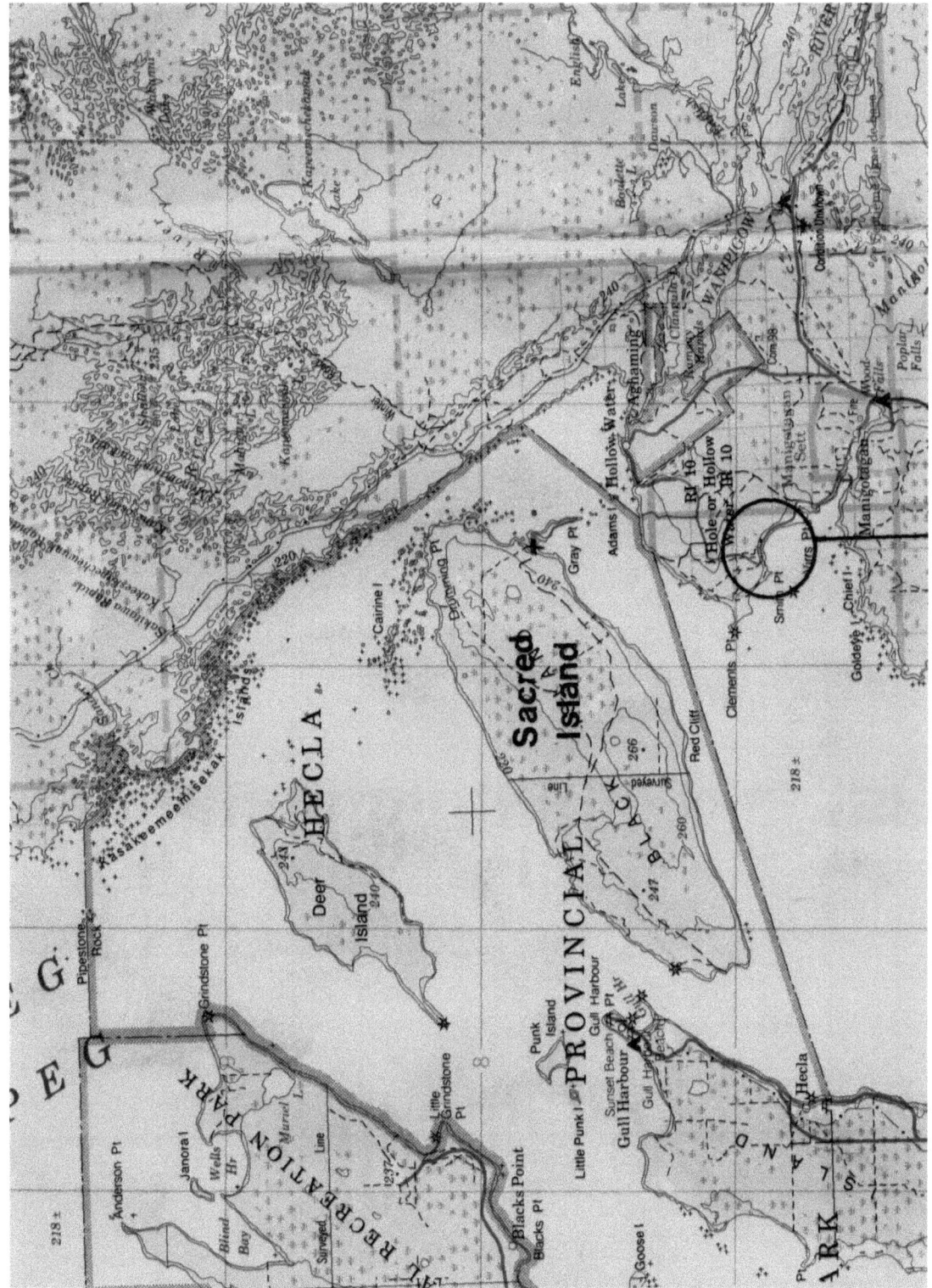

Figure 11: Location of the Rice River Survey Area
(National Topographic Series 1:50000 Map)

The Beaver Creek survey (survey location shown in Figure 12) was not as successful as the Rice River survey for a number of reasons. First, the crew was not accompanied by an Elder; therefore, the survey was designed as a traditional archaeological survey. The survey was a stratified random sample in a number of cut block locations. The crews were hampered by inclement weather, which made much of the study area inaccessible. Access to the study area could only be gained via a dirt logging road which, under rainy conditions, became impassable to vehicles smaller than a logging truck. Despite these drawbacks, the crews were able to dig over 200 test pits, covering some twenty square kilometers of boreal forest. No sites were found during this phase of the field work; however, since many of the cut blocks were located in low potential areas away from major lakes, it was designed to test the littoral bias further.

The 2001 survey accomplished its goals. The importance of the cultural data was re-confirmed, and the strength of that data made apparent by the identification of twenty-two new sites. Furthermore, the Beaver Creek Survey confirmed that areas that were great distances away from lakes or rivers were not likely to contain sites. Therefore, based on two seasons of intensive field testing, it can be safely said that the littoral bias is not artificial and is a real phenomenon.

Both the field crew and the Elder were surprised at how well current and past land-use areas meshed with archaeological sites that were found. Some of the sites found at places identified by the Elder had multiple components that stretched back in time as much as 5000 yrs BP. This clearly shows that land-use patterns may have greater applicability back in time than previously suspected. This would support arguments that post-European contact acculturation did not change basic land-use patterns of First Nations groups in the boreal forest. Rather, change occurred in the way that these groups traveled between points on the seasonal round, with more round trips between the now permanent settlement site and the locations where resources were sought, as suggested the acculturation pattern discovered by Brody (1988).

The two summers of field survey identified a total of forty-three new sites in the study area, which represents an increase of the site database in the study area of almost 25%. It established that the littoral distribution of sites is real. Additionally, it validated the variables selected for the models, especially the power of the cultural variables. The success of each of the models developed for this research in predicting site location is discussed in chapter 7.

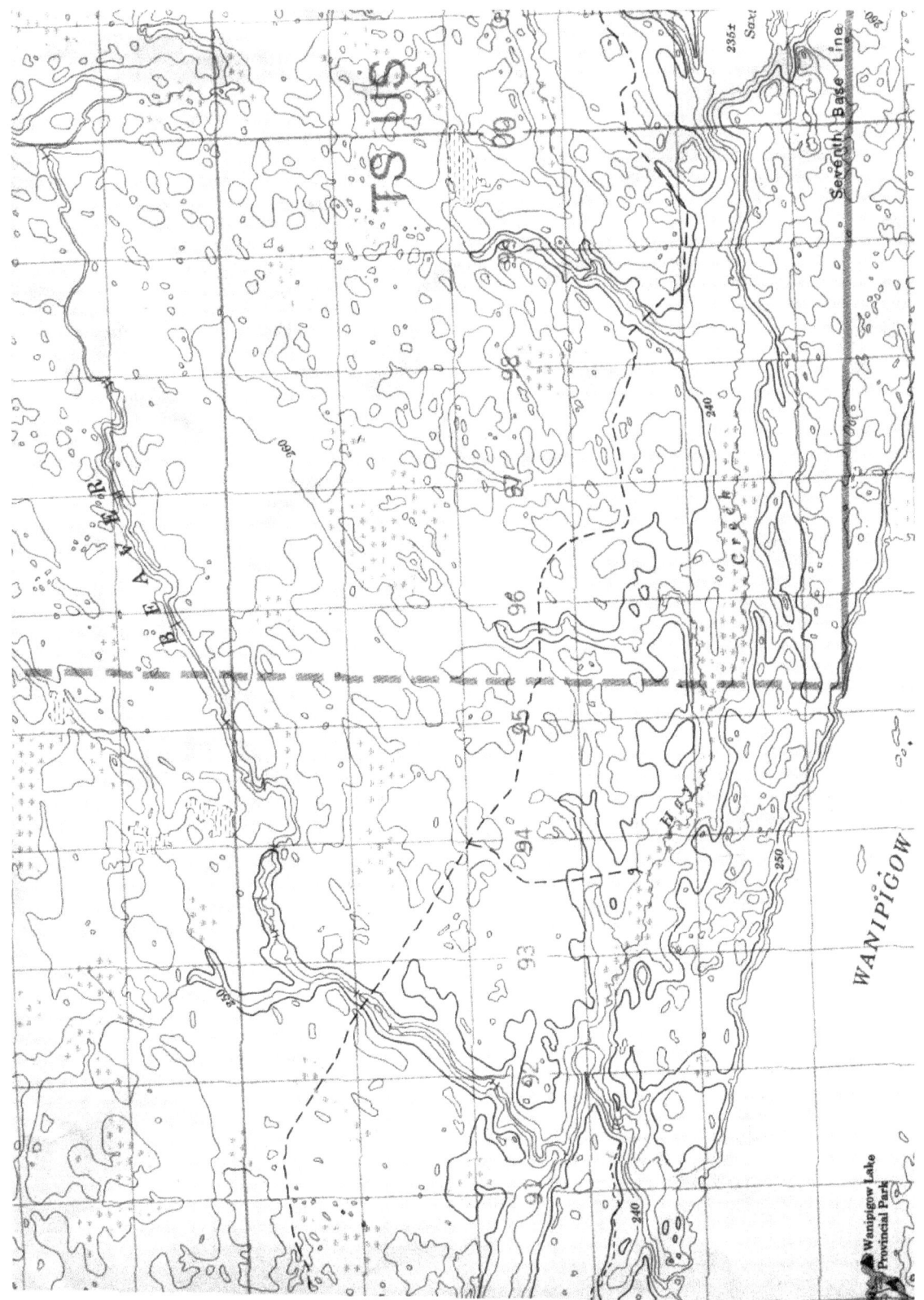

Figure 12: The Location of Beaver Creek
(National Topographic Series Map 1:50000 Scale)

Chapter 7 Results

7.0 Results

The results of the modeling processes are presented in this chapter. The predictive power of each of the models is reviewed individually, using validation methods, discussed in chapter 6.

7.1 Cultural Environmental Model – CARP

It was anticipated that the CARP cultural environmental model would be the weakest of the predictive models created, because it considers each of the variables independently. Since the variables are weighted individually, then combined to create the predictive model score, the CARP method does not act as a true weighted value method, but more as a weighted intersection method. To get a prediction of high archaeological potential enough points must intersect, but is irrespective of the source. It is therefore possible for a site with a high-scoring distance to water, aspect and tree type, but is located on a forty-five degree slope, to receive a high archaeological potential score. Clearly this would not be a logical place to have a site, however.

The CARP cultural-environmental model is shown in Figure 13, and a summary of the results are in Table 2. The class and spot weightings used to create the model are shown in Appendix 3.

This model is a fairly parsimonious predictor; 86.9% of all the cells in the study area are predicted as low in archaeological potential. Eight percent of the cells are classified as areas of medium archaeological potential and only 1.1% are classified as high archaeological potential.

The results of the survey statistic are presented in Table 3. An archaeologist would have to survey approximately 13.14% of the study area to discover 80.25% of the sites used in the creation of the model and 60.71% of the new sites from the 2000 and 2001 survey. While this is a good survey statistic, the difference in the rate of success in predicting original site data and new survey data suggests that there are methodological problems with the CARP methodology (see chapter 8 for discussion).

Table 2: Summary of Results for the CARP Cultural-Environmental Model

	Old Sites	Percent	Cells in Environment	Percent	New Sites	Percent	Non-Sites	Percent
Low Potential	16	0.1975	2015477	0.8687	11	0.3929	68	0.7640
Medium Potential	65	0.8025	279777	0.1206	7	0.2500	21	0.2360
High Potential	0	0.0000	24951	0.0108	10	0.3571	0	0.0000

Table 3: Survey Statistic for CARP Cultural-Environmental Model

	Old Sites	New Sites
Survey Ratio (% of Area:% of Sites)	0.1314:0.8025	0.1314:0.6071

Table 4: Kolmogorov-Smirnov Test Results

	New Sites	Cumulative Percent	Non-Sites	Cumulative Percent	Difference
Low Potential	11	0.3929	68	0.7640	-0.3712
Medium Potential	7	0.6429	21	1.0000	-0.3571
High Potential	10	1.0000	0	1.0000	0.0000

Table 5: Gain Statistic for CARP Cultural-Environmental Model

	Old Sites	New Sites
Gain Statistic	0.8363	0.7836

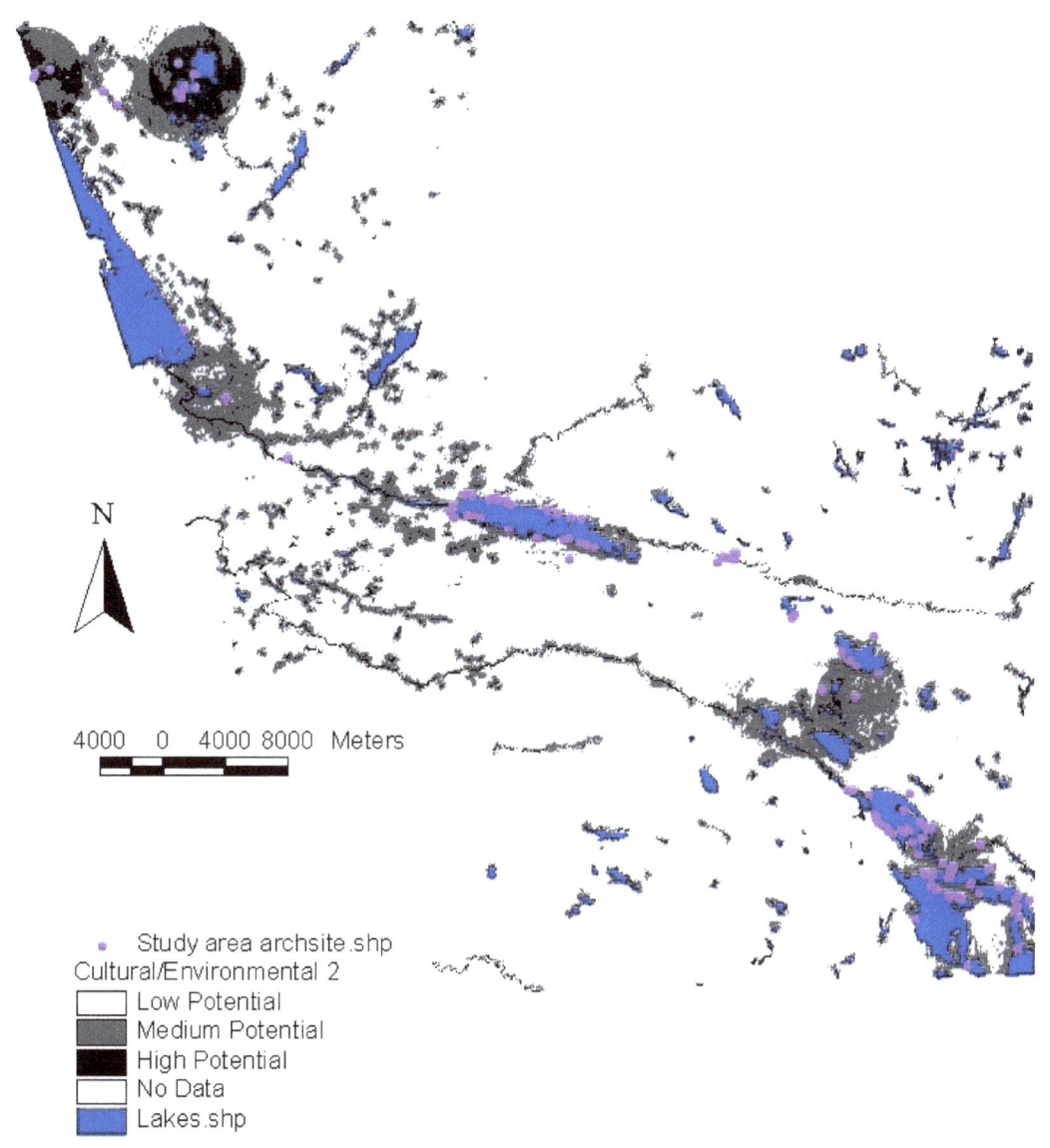

Cultural/Environmental CARP Model

Figure 13: CARP Cultural-Environmental Model

The Kolmogorov-Smirnov test results for new sites and non-sites are presented in Table 4. The D_{max} value for this test is 0.3712, which exceeds the critical value of 0.2570, indicating that there is a statistically significant difference between the predictions for new sites versus non-site random points. The model results, therefore, are significantly better than a random point selection.

The results of the gain statistic calculation are presented in Table 5. Clearly the gain statistic for both old and new sites shows that the model does have some predictive power, although that predictive power is better for sites that were employed in the creation of the model than for the new sites.

Of the new sites resulting from the surveys, thirteen are in areas of low archaeological potential, nine in areas of medium archaeological potential and twelve were classified as high archaeological potential. Sites along the Rice River and Shallow Lake did fairly well in the test, likely because many of these sites are located in areas where cultural data had high predictive scores. Where scores from the land-use data are high, only a few other highly ranked attributes need to intersect the cells to result in high archaeological potential scores.

The CARP cultural-environmental model scores fairly well using the three evaluation criteria. The fact that none of the sites used in building the predictive model had scores sufficiently high to classify them as areas of high archaeological potential suggests that there are methodological problems with this approach, however. These problems will be discussed further in chapter 8.

7.2 Cultural Environmental Model – Logistic Regression

The cultural environmental model is created using the same variables as the CARP model but uses logistic regression to calculate the weights. The weights and the intercept value, calculated by SPSS, are presented in Table 6. The model multiplies each of the variables by their weights and then adds or subtracts the intercept value in the Map Calculator of ArcView. The resultant predictive model is shown in Figure 14.

The model is nearly as parsimonious a predictor as the CARP style model, with 86.1% of all cells in the modeling area scored as areas of low archaeological potential. Only four percent of the cells fall into medium potential. This distribution of potential is of concern, because it seems to indicate that values are polarized between low potential areas and high potential areas. A total of 9.9% of all cells in the study area are classified as having high archaeological potential. The results of the model are summarized in Table 7.

Table 6: Parameter Estimates for Variables

Variable	Weight
Intercept	-11.404
Distance to Lakes	0.006859
Distance to Rivers	-0.01027
Slope	0.05919
Aspect	0.01006
Forest Resource Inventory	0.02007
Distance to Industrial Resources	-0.0008552
Distance to Trails and Cabins	0.0001927
Distance to Ceremonial Resources	0.00000753
Distance to Local Resources	0.0004106
Distance to Faunal Resources	0.0003861
Distance to Earth Resources	0.001077
Distance to Vegetative Resources	0.0008524

Table 7: Summary of Results for Cultural-Environmental Logistic Regression Model

	Old Sites	Percent	Cells in Environment	Percent	New Sites	Percent	Non-Sites	Percent
Low Potential	0	0.0000	1990284	0.8607	18	0.6429	79	0.8876
Medium Potential	1	0.0123	92333	0.0399	0	0.0000	3	0.0337
High Potential	80	0.9877	229857	0.0994	10	0.3571	7	0.0787

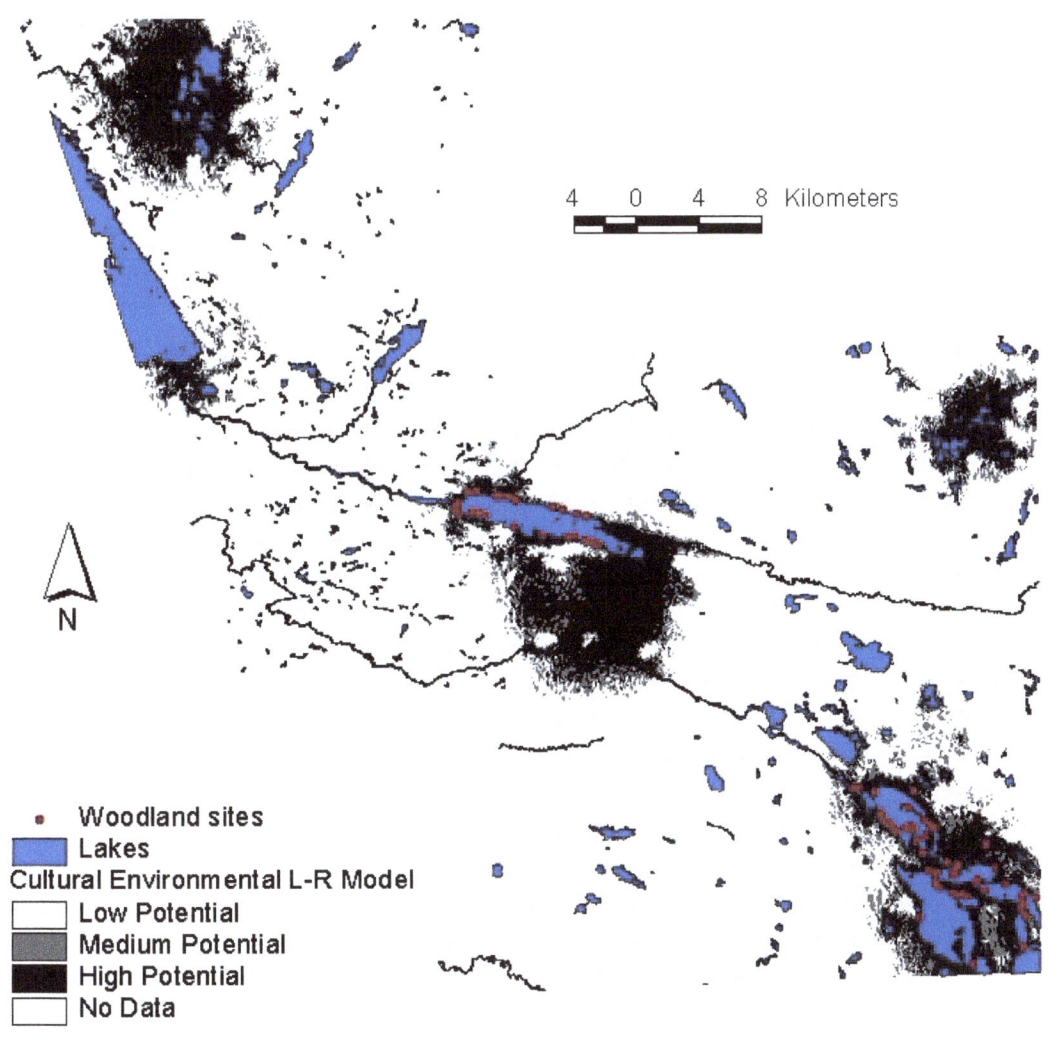

Cultural Environmental Model (Logistic Regression)

Figure 14: Cultural Environmental Model by Logistic Regression

The survey results are somewhat disappointing by comparison. Eighteen of the twenty-eight new sites fall within areas of low archaeological potential. In fact, some of the new sites are located in areas that have a probability of zero of containing an archaeological site. None of the new sites fall within areas of medium potential. Ten of the sites were correctly classified as being in high potential areas.

The results of the survey statistic are presented in Table 8. While the model scores well for the old sites, with a 13.93% study area survey uncovering 100% of the sites, the statistic is much less encouraging for the new sites, with a 13.93% study area survey only discovering 35.71% of the new sites. Clearly this is a much lower result than found with the CARP methodology model for the discovery of new sites.

The results of the Kolmogorov-Smirnov test are shown in Table 9. The D_{max} value for this test is 0.2785, exceeding the critical value of 0.2570. Therefore it can be said that there is a statistically significant difference between the predictions for the new sites versus the non-site random points and the model has predictive power.

The results of the gain statistic calculation are presented in Table 10. The gain statistic for the sites employed in the creation of the model is quite good, at 0.8607, suggesting that the model has good predictive powers. However, for the sites found as a result of the field work, the gain statistic suggests only an average gain of 0.6099.

If one examines the map, it is immediately apparent that the areas of high archaeological potential are focused in regions immediately adjacent to large lakes, containing a majority of the sites employed in the creation of the model. However, unlike the CARP model, there are few areas away from the lakes classified as high potential. This fact may correlate with the relatively poor rate of prediction of the archaeological sites found in the 2000 and 2001 surveys, as demonstrated by the survey statistic for new sites (see discussion, chapter 8).

Table 8: Survey Statistic for Cultural-Environmental Logistic Regression Model

	Old Sites	New Sites
Survey Ratio (% of Area:% of Sites)	0.1393:1	0.1393:0.3571

Table 9: Kolmogorov-Smirnov Test of Significance Results

	New Sites	Cumulative Percent	Non-Sites	Cumulative Percent	Difference
Low Potential	18	0.6429	79	0.8876	-0.2448
Medium Potential	0	0.6429	3	0.9213	-0.2785
High Potential	10	1.0000	7	1.0000	0.0000

Table 10: Gain Statistic for Cultural-Environmental Logistic Regression Model

	Old Sites	New Sites
Gain Statistic	0.8607	0.6099

Table 11: Parameter Estimates for Economic Variables

Variable	Weight
Moose HSI	-.099
Woodland Caribou HSI	-1.180
Intercept Value	.313

7.3 Economic Model – Logistic Regression

The economic model consists of only two variables, the moose Habitat Suitability Index (HSI) and the Woodland Caribou HSI. The parameter estimates for these two variables are shown in Table 11.

Once SPSS has calculated the logistic regression equation, it provides a self-test of the equation. It does so by attempting to predict the data originally used in the calculation, using the calculated regression equation. If a site or non-site is calculated at greater than 0.500, it is considered to be correctly predicted. The results of this self-prediction test are shown in Table 12. Only 52.8% of non-sites were correctly predicted as being non-sites by SPSS. Site locations fared better, with 76.5% of the predictions proving correct. An overall rate of 64.1% of sites and non-sites are correctly predicted by parameter estimates. However, this indicates that the sites and the non-sites are almost indistinguishable in terms of their relationships with the moose and caribou HSI values. This raises immediate concerns about the quality of the model calculated by SPSS and its ability to distinguish sites from non-sites.

The map created by the logistic regression equation is shown in Figure 15. While interesting in terms of the patterns it suggests, the map is not a particularly parsimonious predictor. It does not actually classify any cells as being low in archaeological potential. The majority of the cells are classified as being of medium potential, at 65.8%. The remaining 34.2% of cells are classified as being of high archaeological potential. This clearly reflects the confused nature of the values at site and non-site locations and the difficulty that SPSS had in making a distinction between site and non-site areas. The self-prediction of sites used in the creation of the model also shows a similar pattern. Seventeen of the sites are classified as being in areas of medium potential. The remaining sixty-four sites are classified as being in areas of high archaeological potential. A summary of the results is shown in Table 13.

The survey results are similarly disappointing. Thirty-two of the sites are located in areas of medium archaeological potential. Only two sites are located in areas of high archaeological potential. The economic model is currently not a strong predictor of archaeological site location.

The results of the survey statistic are presented in Table 14. This statistic clearly shows that the model would not be an effective tool for use by archaeologists. In order to survey all the areas of medium and high potential, an archaeologist would be required to survey 100% of the study area (although that would recover 100% of the sites in the region). Therefore, there is nothing upon which to base a survey choice.

The results of the Kolmogorov-Smirnov test are shown in Table 15. The D_{max} value for this test is 0.2769, which exceeds the critical value of 0.2570. Therefore, there is a statistically significant difference between the predictions for the new sites versus the non-site random points and the model has predictive power for site locations. However, the utility of this determination is unclear, because the model clearly is not an effective archaeological tool.

The results of the gain statistic calculation are presented in Table 16. The result of zero for the gain statistic for sites employed in the creation of the model, as well as for sites resulting from the fieldwork suggests that the economic model has little predictive power whatsoever.

The economic model is clearly not an effective tool for the prediction of archaeological site locations. Habitat suitability is too homogeneous to enable a clear distinction between site and non-site areas.

Table 12: Summary of Self-Validation Results by SPSS

		Predicted		Percentage Correct
		RESPONSE		
Observed		Non-Site	Site	
RESPONSE	Non-Site	47	42	52.8
	Site	19	62	76.5
		Overall Percentage		64.1

Table 13: Summary of Results of Economic Logistic Regression Model

	Old Sites	Percent	Cells in Environment	Percent	New Sites	Percent	Non-Site	Percent
Low potential	0	0.0000	0	0.0000	0	0.0000	0	0.0000
Medium potential	17	0.2099	1524806	0.6578	26	0.9286	58	0.6517
High Potential	64	0.7901	793218	0.3422	2	0.0714	31	0.3483

Table 14: Survey Statistic for Economic Logistic Regression Model

	Old Sites	New Sites
Survey Ratio (% of Area:% of Sites)	1:1	1:1

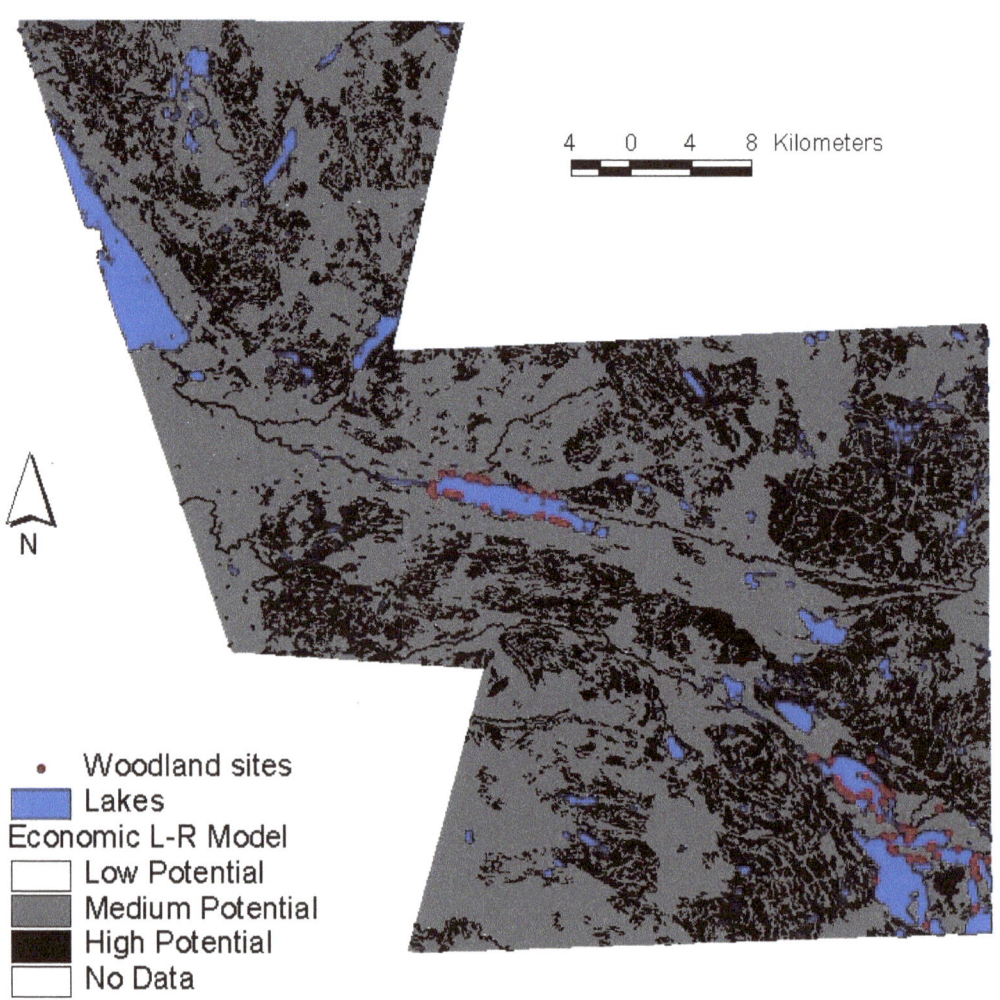

Figure 15: Economic Model by Logistic Regression

Table 15: Kolmogorov-Smirnov Test of Significance Results

	New Sites	Cumulative Percent	Non-Site	Cumulative Percent	Difference
Low potential	0	0.0000	0	0.0000	0.0000
Medium potential	26	0.9286	58	0.6517	0.2769
High Potential	2	1.0000	31	1.0000	0.0000

Table 16: Gain Statistic for Economic Logistic Regression Model

	Old Sites	New Sites
Gain Statistic	0	0

7.4 Cultural-Environmental-Economic Model – Logistic Regression

The final model employs cultural, environmental and economic data. All available variables were analyzed in SPSS, although, as is demonstrated in Table 17, not all variables are correlated strongly enough to be given weights greater than 0.001. Several of the land-use data variables are not strongly correlated enough to get a weighting value. The resultant model is shown in Figure 16.

The model self-validation by SPSS is quite promising, with an overall success rate of 95.1% at predicting site and non-site responses correctly. One hundred percent of site responses were correctly predicted by SPSS in its internal validation, and 92.1% of non-sites were correctly predicted. This is shown in Table 18. A summary of the model results is shown in Table 19.

Unfortunately, the cultural-environmental-economic model is not a parsimonious predictor. Low potential areas only occupy 19.3% of all environmental cells. Medium potential cells comprise another 6.7% of all cells. An astounding 74% of all cells in the environment are classified as being of high archaeological potential. Clearly this extremely high percentage of high potential cells would exclude this combination model as a practical tool for an archaeological application. Not surprisingly, all eighty-one of the sites used in the creation of this model fall into the high potential category.

Four of the new archaeological sites are located in cells that are classified as low potential. The other thirty new sites fall into areas of high archaeological potential. It is somewhat surprising, considering the high percentage of cells in the environment that are high archaeological potential, that any of the new archaeological sites would fall into areas of low archaeological potential.

The results of the survey statistic are presented in Table 20. The statistic clearly shows that this model would not be an effective tool in survey design. Slightly more than 80% of the study area is classified as high or medium potential. This fact alone would disqualify the cultural-environmental-economic model as a serious archaeological tool.

The results of the Kolmogorov-Smirnov test are shown in Table 21. The D_{max} value for this test is 0.1288, which means that it cannot be said that there is a statistically significant difference between the predictions for sites and for non-sites by the cultural-environmental-economic model.

The results of the gain statistic calculation are presented in Table 22. The low gain of 0.1932 for the sites employed in the calculation shows that this model has very little predictive power. The negative gain for new sites shows that the model actually has reverse predictive abilities, in that more of the sites fall outside the areas that are classified as high and medium potential than fall in those areas.

The results of the validation for the cultural-environmental-economic model show that it is a weak model for predicting archaeological site locations. As with the economic model, the high percentage of cells in the study area classified as high potential would disqualify it for use as a tool by archaeologists.

The modeling results are mixed. All of the models have their strengths and weaknesses. A discussion of the relative merits of each of the model types is contained in the following chapter.

Table 17: Parameter Estimates for the Cultural-Environmental-Economic Model

Variable	Weight
Moose HIS	4.069
Woodland Caribou HSI	-.816
Distance to Lakes	-.008
Distance to Rivers	.009
Slope	-.044
Aspect	-.011
Forest Resource Inventory	-.035
Distance to Industrial Resources	.001
Distance to Trails and Cabins	.000
Distance to Ceremonial Resources	.000
Distance to Local Resources	.000
Distance to Faunal Resources	.000
Distance to Earth Resources	-.001
Distance to Vegetative Resources	-.001
Intercept	11.664

Table 18: Model Self-Validation by SPSS

		Predicted		
		RESPONSE		Percentage Correct
Observed		Non-Site	Site	
RESPONSE	Non-Site	82	7	92.1
	Site	0	81	100.0
Overall Percentage				95.9

Table 19: Summary of Results for Cultural-Environmental-Economic Model

	Old Sites	Percent	Cells in Environment	Percent	New Sites	Percent	Non-Sites	Percent
Low Potential	0	0.0000	446918	0.1933	3	0.1071	16	0.1798
Medium Potential	0	0.0000	155074	0.0671	0	0.0000	5	0.0562
High Potential	81	1.0000	1710338	0.7397	25	0.7353	68	0.7640

Table 20: Survey Statistic for Cultural-Environmental-Economic Logistic Regression Model

	Old Sites	New Sites
Survey Ratio (% of Area:% of Sites)	0.8068:1	0.8068:0.7353

Table 21: Kolmogorov-Smirnov Test of Significance Results

	New Sites	Cumulative Percent	Non-Sites	Cumulative Percent	Difference
Low Potential	3	0.1071	16	0.1798	-0.0726
Medium Potential	0	0.1071	5	0.2360	-0.1288
High Potential	25	1.0000	68	1.0000	0.0000

Table 22: Gain Statistic for Cultural-Environmental-Economic Logistic Regression Model

	Old Sites	New Sites
Gain Statistic	0.1932	-0.0972

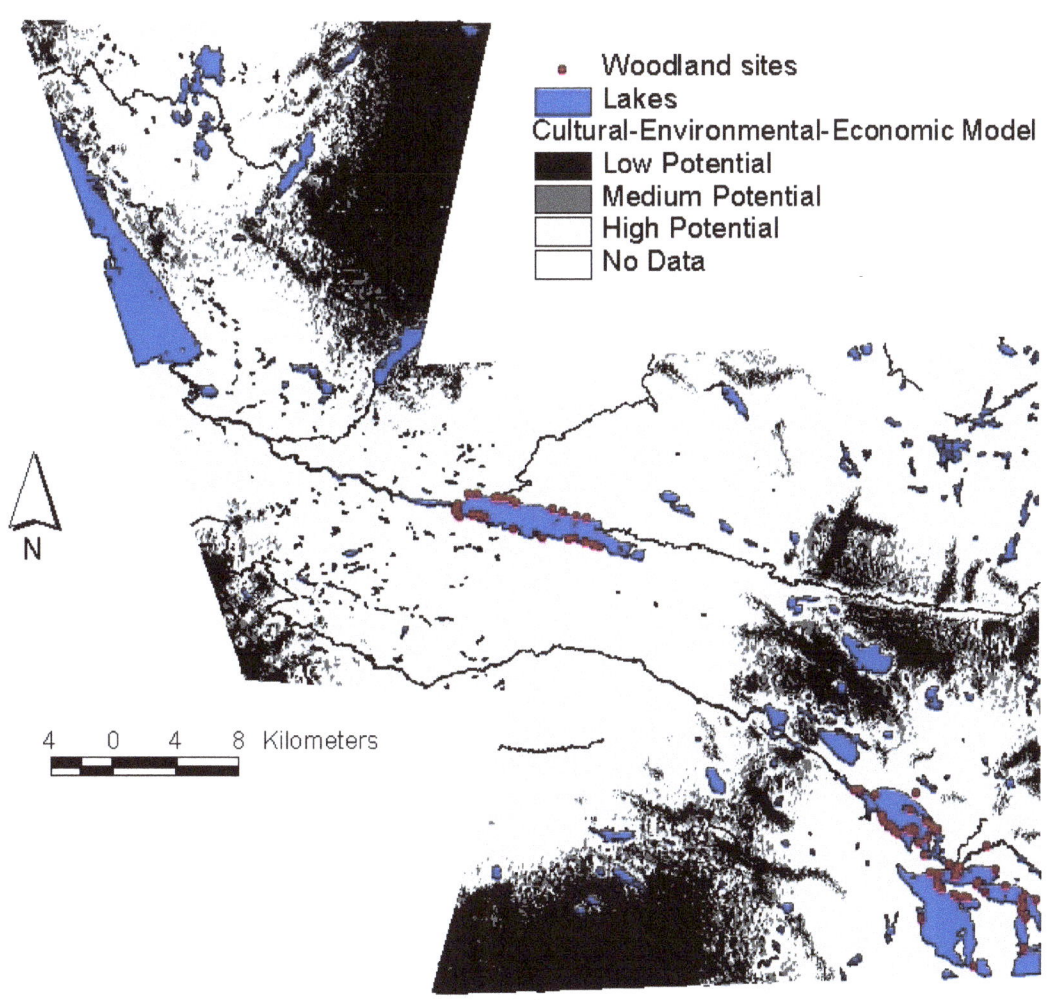

Figure 16: Cultural-Environmental-Economic Model by Logistic Regression

Chapter 8 Discussion of Results

8.0 Discussion of Results

This chapter discusses the model results presented in chapter 7. The four models presented in chapter 7 are compared using three evaluation tools: the survey statistic, the Kolmogorov-Smirnov test of statistical significance and the gain statistic. The efficacy of the models is evaluated using these tools. The models' relative predictive abilities are evaluated below. This evaluation allows for comment on the modeling methods themselves. Finally, the research goals are evaluated.

8.1 Survey Statistic Evaluation

The survey statistic is designed to evaluate the percentage of cells in the study area that fall into medium and high archaeological potential classes and the percentage of sites that would be found if those areas were surveyed. The statistic is calculated for the sites used in the creation of the models, as well as for the sites found as a result of the field work. The survey statistic results for the four model types are summarized in Table 23.

The first thing that is evident in examining the survey statistic is that the economic and cultural-environmental economic models are parsimonious; the number of cells contained in areas of high and medium potential in these models are 100% and 80% respectively. This disqualifies these models as serious archaeological tools, so they can be excluded from consideration on the basis of the survey statistic alone.

The CARP cultural-environmental and the cultural-environmental models are almost identical in terms of the area that would have to be surveyed if all areas of medium and high potential were given 100% coverage. The CARP model is not as efficient at finding the sites that were originally used in the creation of the model, however; only 80.25% occur in high and medium potential areas, compared to the cultural-environmental model's rate of 100%. Unfortunately, 0% of the sites are located in areas of high potential in the CARP model, which casts doubts on the methodology. The results for the discovery of new sites are clearly in favour of the CARP model, however. A survey of high and medium potential regions as identified by the CARP model would result in the discovery of 60% of the new sites, as compared to 35% using the logistic regression model. Methodological concerns aside, the CARP model appears more powerful than the logistic regression model. However, the way in which the survey would be structured would be a factor in this case. In addition to the lake shore regions, the CARP model would require the survey of a number of isolated land parcels predicted as being high potential. This is a logistically costly survey because it would be necessary to move archaeological crews from one area to another. In comparison, the logistic regression model views many of the areas of interest as contiguous, which facilitates survey.

Table 23: Survey Statistic Summary (% of Area:% of Sites)

	Old Sites	New Sites
CARP Cultural-Environmental Model	0.1314:0.8025	0.1314:0.6071
Cultural-Environmental Logistic Regression Model	0.1393:1	0.1393:0.3571
Economic Logistic Regression Model	1:1	1:1
Cultural-Environmental-Economic Logistic Regression Model	0.8068:1	0.8068:0.7353

Table 24: Summary of Kolmogorov-Smirnov Testing Results

Model	D_{max} Value
CARP Cultural-Environmental Model	0.3712
Cultural-Environmental Logistic Regression Model	0.2785
Economic Logistic Regression Model	0.2769
Cultural-Environmental-Economic Logistic Regression Model	0.1288

Table 25: Gain Statistic Summary

	Gain Statistic		
Model	Old Sites	New Sites	Average Gain
CARP Cultural-Environmental Model	0.8363	0.7836	0.80995
Cultural-Environmental Logistic Regression Model	0.8607	0.6099	0.7353
Economic Logistic Regression Model	0	0	0
Cultural-Environmental-Economic Logistic Regression Model	0.1932	-0.0972	0.048

8.2 Kolmogorov-Smirnov Testing

The Kolmogorov-Smirnov test is designed to detect significant differences between the frequencies of two variables, as discussed in chapter 2. Here, the test is used to determine whether there is a significant difference between the predictions made for sites resulting from the fieldwork and non-site random points generated for the creation of the models, as discussed in chapter 6. In the Kolmogorov Smirnov test, the critical value must be exceeded in order for the results to be significant at the 0.05 level of significance. The formula for the critical value (shown in chapter 2) calculates the critical value for the target region as 0.2570, at a 0.05 level of significance. If the critical value is exceeded, then the alternative hypothesis (that there is a significant difference between the predictions of archaeological significance for site versus for non-sites) can be accepted. If the critical value is not exceeded, then thenull hypothesis (there is no significant difference between the predictions for sites and non-sites) must be accepted. The results of the Kolmogorov-Smirnov testing for each of the models are summarized in table 24.

The D_{max} value for the CARP cultural-environmental, the cultural-environmental logistic regression and the economic models exceed the critical value. Therefore, it can be said that each of these models are significant in predicting site versus non-site locations. The fourth model, the cultural-environmental-economic logistic regression model, is not statistically significant in terms of the predictions for sites and non-sites. The economic model has already been rejected as a tool for archaeologists, on the basis of the survey statistic. Although the D_{max} value for the CARP model exceeds the critical value by more than the cultural-environmental logistic regression model, the Kolmogorov-Smirnov statistic cannot be read in such a manner to suggest that this is a more powerful model.

8.3 Gain Statistic Evaluation

The gain statistic, as introduced by Kvamme (1988a), is a measure of what is gained using the predictive power of the model. It compares of the percentage of the study area deemed to be high and medium potential compared to the percentage of sites found in those regions, as discussed in chapter 6. Here, gain statistics are calculated for the sites employed in the creation of the models and the sites found as a result of the field work. These two gain statistics are averaged to provide an overall gain for the models. The summary of the statistics for each of the models is shown in table 25.

The economic and the cultural-environmental-economic models are shown to be very poor predictors. The gain of 0 for the economic model means that it has no predictive power whatsoever, and the very small overall gain of the cultural-environmental-economic model means that it has little predictive power. The negative gain means that the cultural-environmental-economic model would actually have reverse predictive power.

The predictive power of the two cultural-environmental models is of interest in terms of their gain scores. The gain for sites used in the creation of the models is almost identical (0.8363 for the CARP model and 0.8607 for the logistic regression model). The gains are different for the models in terms of the sites found as a result of the fieldwork, however, with the CARP model scoring higher. These differences are averaged through the overall gain, which is 0.80995 for the CARP model and 0.7353 for the logistic regression model. Although this indicates that the CARP model is the better of the two in terms of its predictive power, this power may be more apparent than real, as discussed in the following section.

Based on the evaluation tools, it is apparent that the economic and the cultural-environmental-economic models are weak and should not be adopted by archaeologists designing surveys. The CARP model is more powerful than the cultural-environmental logistic regression model in terms of its overall score.

8.4 Evaluation of Modeling Methods

Two modeling methods are employed in this research – the CARP method (a weighted intersection method) and logistic regression (a weighted value method). The final results of the evaluation testing of the models are somewhat mixed. Both of these approaches to modeling have some attractive aspects, but neither of these models contained all of the desired characteristics of an effective archaeological predictive model.

Both models are parsimonious, with less than a 1% difference between them. The CARP model was extremely poor at self-validation, however, and none of the sites used in the creation of the model fell in cells classified as high archaeological potential, despite the fact that all were Woodland sites. This failure suggests that there is a methodological flaw in the CARP protocol, which suggests in turn that it may not be as efficient a predictor as the statistical results suggest.

The flaw in the CARP methodology may stem from the fact that each of the variables must be divided into discrete classes in order to be analyzed and weighted. Some of these classes can be derived from logical divisions in the variable itself. For example, the variable "aspect" (discussed in chapter 6) can employ the cardinal compass directions as the discrete classes. For some variables, the divisions into discrete classes are more arbitrary, which opens the process to error. Furthermore, the use of discrete classes may hide variation in the data. With logistic regression, continuous values of the variables are employed in the creation of the model, avoiding this potential source of error.

A second drawback to the CARP methodology is an outgrowth of the first, in that the CARP method requires more steps to create a model. Computation time is increased due to the preparation of data and the creation of discrete variable classes. This drawback is minimized when logistic regression is used as an alternative.

A third drawback of the CARP method, as discussed in Chapter 7, is that it cannot be considered a true weighted value method. Ranks of high archaeological potential result from the intersection of an adequate number of points from the predictor variables. The intersection of variables can happen even in areas where sites would not be located, such as steep slopes. Since the variables are considered and weighted in isolation, areas that would be totally undesirable otherwise can become ranked as high in archaeological potential through the intersection of highly ranked predictors, rather than their simultaneous occurrence. This phenomenon can bee seen in Figure 7-1, where many areas isolated from water sources are ranked as high potential. Furthermore, since variable weights are determined both by subjective and objective means (see chapter 7), this leaves the model open to manipulations by the archaeologist in the creation of the model. It is certainly tempting, when so many sites are poorly self-predicted, to go back through the process and manipulate the weights in order to change the trend. However, such a manipulation would be an unfair test of the CARP methodology.

Logistic regression appears to be a more robust modeling method, as it does not suffer from the problems identified above. It also poses some concerns, however. The method is a relatively parsimonious predictor, but the nature of the variables is an important factor in the predictions. Furthermore, the logistic regression model appears to be less powerful as a tool for predicting new sites (Table 23 and 25). However, it is capable of self-prediction (Table 23 and 25) where CARP showed some weaknesses, and it placed sites in high values cells which CARP did not. This ability suggests that logistic regression is more sound methodologically. The logistic regression method is much more powerful in self-prediction of the sites employed in the creation of the models. This might seem self-evident, but the CARP model shows that self-prediction is not always a given.

Another advantage of logistic regression is that the predictions are expressed as probability scores, ranging from 0 to 1, rather than as arbitrary sums in the CARP method. Presentation and interpretation of the results of logistic regression are much easier than with the CARP method as a result. A prediction of 0.9882 probability by logistic regression is quickly understood when compared to a predictive score of 147, as might be obtained from the CARP model.

Logistic regression seems to be a more desirable method than the CARP protocol due to the methodological concerns discussed above, despite the its drawbacks (relative weakness of new site prediction). This research does not suggest that logistic regression should be abandoned. For its methodological superiority, logistic regression should be employed and developed further (in attempts to improve its power). It is likely that the logistic regression model is weaker in the prediction of the new sites due to the patchwork coverage of the cultural data variables. Many of the new sites classified as being in low archaeological potential are in the Rice Lake area, for which there is very little cultural data. Since logistic regression is using all the variables simultaneously to make the predictions, areas where data coverage is incomplete are likely to reflect that incompleteness in the archaeological potential probabilities. The CARP methodology, which considers each variable individually and potential is arrived at through an intersection, avoids the problem of unequal data coverage better than logistic regression.

8.5 Evaluation of Predictor Variables

Based on the discussion above, it is clear that cultural and environmental data used in combination are more powerful predictors of site location than economic data, either alone or in combination. There are advantages to extending the "traditional" environmental variables to include cultural land-use data (see results). Land-use data helps to identify areas employed in the seasonal round that might be selected for reasons that are "non-environmental", such as the location of lithic sources or ceremonial resources. While lithic sources can be identified geologically, they are considered cultural in this research because they are ethnographically known to be resources. They may also be considered as cultural data, because people selected certain lithic sources as desirable resources. However, as discussed in chapter 2, while the community of Hollow Water is currently in the process of collecting additional land-use information from elders in their community, only a limited data set was available for this research. This incomplete collection has meant that certain areas have more data than others, which has made the resultant predictions somewhat uneven. As discussed above, this factor is probably the cause of the eighteen new sites to be in areas of low archaeological potential as predicted by the cultural-environmental logistic regression model.

Cultural data is of crucial importance in predicting sites that are used for the extraction of resources or for ceremonial purposes; these sites will not have the same environmental characteristics as the majority of other sites. Thus, cultural data helps archaeologists to understand the totality of the land-use patterns by hunter-gatherer groups. Furthermore, as greater amounts of land-use data are collected, they may help archaeologists to determine what discriminates one area of high archaeological potential from another. In the future, archaeological predictive models of the study region will be better able to predict site locations because more cultural data are collected.

The results from the economic variable analyses are not encouraging. The economic variables do not differentiate site and non-site areas clearly enough. Other research (e.g. Krist and Brown, 1994) indicates that economic factors can be important variables in site selection. The failure of the economic variables may be explained due to three factors. First, it could be a function of the initial set of sites being grouped together regardless of function. That is, the models are created using all archaeological sites, regardless of whether the site was a campsite, a kill site or it served some other purpose. Sites of different function are normally grouped together in traditional predictive modeling. This is often due to the fact the function of a site cannot easily be determined, especially in the boreal forest, where preservation of organic remains is low, leaving mostly lithics and features as the main evidence of a site. While this is potentially a problem for all types of model, it is of particular concern for the economic model, which is focusing solely on subsistence and site location in its relation to subsistence practices. Sites of different function would have had very different criteria determining their location. If the sites located in areas where the woodland caribou habitat suitability has a score of one are caribou kill sites, it may be confirmation that the suitability index can be used to correctly predict kill site locations and would support the creation of separate models for different site functions. However, there are problems with the adoption of functionality divisions in the creation of models, especially in the boreal forest. It is often impossible to determine site function based on the artifacts found in sites. The highly acidic soils of the boreal forest do not favour the preservation of bone, which adds to the difficulties in determining site function. This point is reinforced by the results of the 2000 survey, where all but the historic sites were indeterminate in terms of their cultural affiliation and function.

Second, the failure of the economic models may be due to the important ecological differences between the modern, managed forest and the pre-contact forest. The side effects of managing forests and protecting forests from fires have changed the dynamics of the forest, especially the understory. For archaeologists, some understanding is required of how this management has affected wildlife populations and ethology in order to use economic variables. The management of the forest has two implications – it affects succession and therefore the distribution of food resources for the animals. On the other hand, the way in which the forest is harvested may, in fact, cancel these concerns, because the process of logging may mimic the way in which pre-contact forests were dynamic and in a constant state of renewal. The use of the habitat suitability index, as a snapshot of habitat suitability from 1987, may not be applicable in pre-contact times, given forestry management.

The third possibility is moose and woodland caribou habitat suitability is rather high and undifferentiated across the study area. If there are many areas of high suitability for moose and for woodland caribou, how do hunter-gatherers select those areas that they will focus upon for hunting? Boreal forest hunter-gatherers, dependent upon moose and woodland caribou as major subsistence resources, would have had sophisticated knowledge of places of high hunting suitability and of prey behaviour. Therefore, if the entire available habitat is suitable for prey, it is likely that prey habitat suitability is only part of the factor in determining site location. Other ethological factors would have been considered by the hunter-gatherers, such as the predictability of prey behaviour in breeding grounds and near watering holes.

Despite the disappointments of this first attempt to model economic variables in the boreal forest, I would argue that the experiment should not end here. Although it is ethnographically known that moose and caribou were important species, other economic variables (*e.g.* fish and small game) should be created to help the discrimination of sites from non-sites. Moose and caribou models were chosen for this research not only due to their ethnographically documented importance in traditional economies but also due to the fact that validated models of moose and caribou habitats were available for the study region. A possible alternative is to convert these habitat suitability indices to a type of hunting suitability index, which could reflect the sophisticated prey behaviour knowledge of the boreal forest hunter-gatherers.

One potential problem in the use of the cultural variables is the use of Euclidean, or straight line, distance measures. Movement through the boreal forest can be quite difficult, and there are costs to movement. A possible solution to this problem is the calculation of cost, or friction, surfaces. This may be a better approach to modeling the cost of movement through the boreal forest than the straight distances employed in this analysis. Cost surfaces assign weights to each cell in a map, associated with the cost of movement through that cell (Douglas, 1994, van Leusen, 1999). Generally, cost surfaces are related to the steepness of the slope, based on the slope theme. In a cost surface, slope values are given a relative cost, representing the energy required to move through each cell in the cost surface. Distances are calculated as least-cost paths between a starting point and a destination. There are several reasons, however, why this approach was not adopted here. First, movement through the boreal forest is more complex than just moving up or down slopes. Other factors, such as vegetation density, water routes and microtopography have to be taken into account. The data do not support the determination of either vegetation density or microtopography. The elevation survey provided for this research is far more accurate than what could be gathered from a 1:50000 National Topographic Series map, but it still masks a great deal of variation (on a scale below the sampling interval). A second factor in the decision not to adopt a cost surface is the fact that other studies (e.g. Bell and Lock, 2000, Harris, 2000, Llobera, 2000) suggest that simple friction surfaces cannot account for actual path decisions made by humans. A least-cost path solution assumes perfect knowledge of the environment. This means that a least cost path would require the individual to know the exact cost of taking a specific path, as well as the costs of every alternative path in order to choose the least-cost path. However, when selecting one path or another, the ultimate cost of that path is unknown at the time of selection. Much like optimal foraging theory, optimality in human travel costs can also be questioned.

The research has shown that locational decisions in the boreal forest are based on a complex set of criteria involving both environmental and cultural aspects of the physical environment and access to local resources, as shown by the variables selected for the cultural-environmental models (see chapter 7). Predictive modeling can only improve through the adoption of more types of data on which to base predictions.

8.6 Evaluation of Research Goals

It is now possible to evaluate the main goals of this study, as identified in chapter 1, based on the results from the models. These goals involved the evaluation of modeling methodology, the examination of predictor variables, and the adoption of general ecological approaches.

8.6.1 Modeling Methodology

For methodological reasons it is suggested that logistic regression is more robust than the CARP methodology, despite differences in predictive power. However, logistic regression should not be accepted uncritically as the best modeling method. The approach is shown to have weaknesses (*e.g.* the relatively low power when predicting new sites) but is considered to be less methodologically suspect.

This research demonstrates some problems with the use of logistic regression. For example, the completeness of coverage of the variables employed in the modeling can cause problems. Despite problems with data coverage, as discussed in previous sections, predictive modeling can still be done and still result in significant predictions.

8.6.2 Predictor Variables

The relative utility of the various predictor variables is assessed above. Environmental and cultural variables in tandem are powerful predictors of site locations and their usefulness is reflected in the relative efficacy of the models completed for this research.

The utility of economic predictor variables used in this research (*i.e.* habitat suitability indices) is shown to be negligible. It is clear that models dependent on only two economic variables are poor predictors of site location. The number of predictor variables beyond the small set of variables offered in this research should be expanded. Only through further experimentation with economic factors will archaeologists be able to definitively determine whether economic factors are or are not good predictors of archaeological site locations.

Does the failure of the economic variables selected to build useful and effective predictive models for the boreal forest have any implications for optimal foraging theory? Likely, yes. In the boreal forest, the patches are extensively distributed and there are many areas that are of high suitability for both moose and woodland caribou habitat, as shown in the maps of moose and caribou habitat in Appendix 6. While optimal foraging theory may predict accurately what patches should be employed in regions where patches are clearly defined and clearly differentiated, it does not seem to have the same power in areas where patches are large or poorly defined. This is demonstrated by the failure of the economic variables to predict site locations. Central place foraging may be useful in the analysis of the trip from a home base to a foraging patch and back, it is only a factor when the location of the related home base and patch are known. Where the relationship between the patch and the home base is unknown, as in the present survey, it becomes impossible using central place foraging to determine if, in fact, a site is located optimally in relation to a patch or patches. This is the case especially when the environment contains a number of patches that have equal utility as in the boreal forest. In sum, OFT fails to provide economic models that adequately model, from an archaeological point of view, hunter-gatherer settlement patterns in the study region.

8.6.3 Ecological Approaches to Modeling

Ecological variables, both in the form of environmental variables and the heavily resource-dominated land-use data, have been shown to be powerful predictors of site location when combined with cultural data. European archaeologists argue that predictive modeling is a form of environmental determinism, but there can be no denying that an ecological or environmental approach to predictive modeling does, in fact, work (*i.e.* it enables archaeologists to predict site location). Admittedly, it is not possible to determine exactly why this approach works, which is a grave weakness. The success of the method is probably related to the fact that people still want to locate near resources.

On balance, results of this research suggests that logistic regression using cultural-environmental variables such as slope, aspect, tree type, distance to lakes/rivers, vegetative resources, ceremonial resources, faunal resources and earth resources can be employed to create powerful archaeological predictive models, which can, in turn, be used for cultural resource management and the design of archaeological survey.

Chapter 9 Conclusion

9.0 Conclusion

Several conclusions can be drawn from this research, especially with respects to the use of archaeological predictive modeling (APM), as highlighted in chapter 8. In chapter 1, three reasons for critically examining APM were offered, including for: 1) APM to protect heritage resources, 2) a critical evaluation of modeling methods and 3) the examination of new predictor variables outside of the usual environmental variables used in the modeling process. This research also has wider implications for the discipline of anthropology generally and the practice of archaeology and APM in particular, as well as for the management of heritage resources by, and for, First Nations communities and forestry companies.

9.1 Implications for Heritage Resource Protection

Archaeologists currently have an incomplete knowledge of the location of heritage resources in the boreal forest and this knowledge may never be complete. The boreal forest covers immense areas in Manitoba and Canada. When the amount of resource extraction that is conducted in the boreal forest is considered, the need for tools to focus archaeological survey is apparent. In order to fully protect heritage resources, archaeologists must work with natural resource companies to build methods and employ tools, such as APM, that will mitigate the impact of natural resource extraction techniques on archaeological deposits.

APM is a tool that can accomplish this goal, and which can be incorporated into the planning processes of natural resources companies. In the case of the forestry industry, these plans are formulated on a very long term basis. Conceivably, with an APM, archaeologists could be sent to harvesting locations well before the first tree was ever cut.

A logistic regression methodology is suggested, employing cultural and environmental datasets, based on the modeling results and methodological considerations. Data availability varies from place to place, but slope, aspect and distance to lake/river themes are universally available. Additional variables, such as soil type, surficial geology or vegetation data can be incorporated as available. For cultural data, the ethnographic record can be critically analyzed to indicate places in the study area which might have been important to pre-contact inhabitants. A logistic regression model run using these data sets will result in the archaeological potential maps. As suggested by the survey statistic in chapters 7 and 8, 100% coverage surveys can be conducted in all areas of high potential. A large proportion (suggested minimum 70%) of the medium archaeological potential could also be included in the survey. Additionally, a smaller stratified sample of low potential areas should also be surveyed (minimally at least 10%). The exact percentages of coverage depend greatly on the size of the study area and the time and resources available for survey.

9.2 Evaluation of Predictive Modeling

This research has shown that APM in the context of hunter-gatherer groups can be an effective and powerful tool. It may indeed be a form of environmental determinism, but it does seem to aid in the analysis of hunter-gatherer settlement patterns. While this does not necessarily explain the nature of the settlement pattern, it is a pattern recognition tool which can provide powerful results.

9.3 Evaluation of Predictor Variables

Different predictor variables were tested in this research through the use of parallel models. This test demonstrated that cultural variables influence site locations, especially for particular types of site, like ceremonial or resource extraction sites. While the strength of the effect depended on the individual variable, as shown by the fact that some of the variables dropped out of the cultural-environmental-economic model, several of the cultural variables have a statistically significant influence on the predictions. The test of economic variables was not as clear. It is possible that the addition of more economic variables would provide a more definitive test of the usefulness of economic variables in APM. The particular economic variable themes chosen (*i.e.* moose and woodland caribou) made it difficult for the statistical test to differentiate between sites and non-sites. The full potential of economic variables remains unresolved, but the difficulties presented by: 1) the boreal forest environment and 2) palaeoenvironmental reconstructions reduce the practicality of incorporating them into archaeological predictive models.

9.4 Implications for the Discipline

The implications of this research for the wider field of anthropology are twofold. First, this research shows the value of cultural ecological approaches in the analysis of human behaviour – particularly settlement patterns. By using environmental variables, as well as cultural aspects of the environment, APM can be considered a cultural ecological approach to the analysis of settlement systems. Sites are shown to be predictable using models that incorporate natural and cultural aspects of the environment.

Another implication of this research for anthropology as a discipline is that land-use patterns, even among "acculturated" groups, can have considerable time depth. The survey of the summer of 2001 with an Elder from the community of Hollow Water demonstrated that information about the local environment, internalized by members of an "acculturated" traditional group, is applicable much deeper in time than previously thought. The nature of this knowledge suggests that there is not necessarily a conscious link between the patterns that contemporary people are following and past settlement patterns. Rather, patterns of land-use are handed down from generation to generation, until conscious knowledge is lost of how deep the patterns may extend. Anthropologists and archaeologists, to see if this discovery holds for other cultures and in other environments, should undertake further examination of the archaeological application of cultural information obtained from Elders by archaeologists.

Finally, this research provides a critical test of two different approaches to modeling. The comparison of the CARP method (a weighted intersection method) and logistic regression (a weighted value method) provides a clear assessment of the strengths and weaknesses of these two very different modeling methodologies. Because the comparison was done on the same dataset, the results can be directly compared, which is one of the strengths of this research. The CARP methodology provides a relatively parsimonious predictive model, but it has some methodological flaws, which makes its apparent predictive strength suspect. Logistic regression is comparable in its efficacy as a predictor, and is a simpler method to implement. Logistic regression does not require as many steps to prepare the data, although it requires outside statistical software.

Optimal foraging theory (OFT) was tested indirectly through the creation of the economic model. Despite the paucity of economic variables (a weakness of this research), the failure of the economic model and the cultural-environmental-economic model to predict site locations accurately has serious implications for OFT. OFT might work well in environments where patches are clearly defined and clearly differentiated, but it fails as an effective tool where those patches are more generalized, or patch sizes are very large. Furthermore, though central place foraging might be a useful tool where site locations and patches are known and can be analyzed for their optimal location, the relationship between archaeological site locations and past resource distributions is unknown and probably cannot be known.

9.5 Implications of the Study for Other Groups

The benefit of this research for First Nations communities goes far beyond the nine jobs provided for high school students over two summers, and beyond the community of Hollow Water. First Nations benefit from this examination of cultural data and the demonstration of its applicability in deep time. For some members of First Nations communities, the results of this test may not come as a surprise, but this research provides evidence which should be used by other anthropologists to show the potential time depth of traditional land-use information. Other benefits to First Nations communities may include, but are not limited to: 1) pride in the strengths of their traditional knowledge; 2) confirmation of the detailed and useful knowledge of the land and its stewardship and exploitation; 3) strengthened connection to the land and 4) land claims evidence.

Cynics may suggest that the ultimate field survey design is not the result of an archaeological predictive model, but rather is achieved by having an Elder accompany archaeological field crews on survey. This approach is not really a valid alternative, however. An individual viewpoint provides no generalizations beyond the specific context of that individual's knowledge. A trapper may know his/her area well, but he/she cannot provide information about other areas. By contrast, the archaeologist can create protocols for the analysis of the ethnographic and ethnohistoric record in order to extract valuable cultural data for use in APM.

This research has provided a tool for use in the planning process of the forestry industry. This research has shown that, while a model created using CARP methodology can make robust predictions, it is more methodologically sound and almost as powerful to use logistic regression.

9.6 Directions for Future Research

One of the areas for future research is the testing of additional economic variables. While the models created using economic variables were poor predictors, as shown by the evaluation tools, it is possible that other variables may not have the same flaws. Also, the application of cultural data in APM should be further investigated and expanded. This research was limited to cultural aspects of the environment, such as the availability of natural resources. Further investigation of other types of cultural data, such as place names and oral traditions, should be done when and where available.

Further research should also be done to assess the impact of forestry practices on subsurface archaeological sites to determine what practices impact archaeological resources the least. Certain practices, like winter cutting, may be acceptable in areas of high archaeological potential because they may have negligible subsurface impacts, although this remains to be proven.

The benefits and implications of this research are clear. APM is a useful tool for 1) the protection of heritage resources, especially in large study areas, 2) a tool for the analysis and prediction of settlement patterns and 3) a tool that can be used to create archaeological survey strategies.

References Cited

Aldenderfer, M. (1991) *The Analytical Engine: Computer Simulations and Archaeological Research* IN: Schiffer, M. B., ed. *Archaeological Method and Theory.* The University of Arizona Press, Tuscon, pp. 195-247.

Allen, K. M. S. (1996) *Iroquoian Landscapes: People, Environments, and the GIS Context* IN: Maschner, H. D. G., ed. *New Methods, Old Problems: Geographic Information Systems in Modern Archaeological Research.* Center for Archaeological Investigations, Southern Illinois University, Carbondale, pp. 198-222.

Altschul, J. (1988) *Models and the Modeling Process* IN: Judge, W. J. and Sebastian, L., eds. *Quantifying the present and predicting the past: Theory, method and application of archaeological predictive modeling.* Government Printing Office, Washington, D. C., pp. 61-96.

Altschul, J. (1990) *Red flag models: the use of modeling in management contexts* IN: Allen, K. M. S., Green, S. W. and Zubrow, E. B. W., eds. *Interpreting space: GIS and archaeology.* Taylor and Francis, London, pp. 226-238.

Alvard, M. (1995) *Intraspecific Prey Choice by Amazonian Hunters. Current Anthropology,* 36, 789-818.

Begossi, A. (1992) *The Use of Optimal Foraging Theory in the Understanding of Fishing Strategies: A Case from Sepetiba Bay (Rio de Janeiro State, Brazil). Human Ecology,* 20, 463-475.

Bell, T. and Lock, G. (2000) *Topographic and cultural influences on walking the Ridgeway in later prehistoric times* IN: Lock, G., ed. *Beyond the Map: Archaeology and Spatial Technologies.* IOS Press, Amsterdam, pp. 85-100.

Belovsky, G. E. (1987) *Hunter-Gatherer Foraging: A Linear Programming Approach. Journal of Anthropological Archaeology,* 6, 29-76.

Belovsky, G. E. (1988) *An Optimal Foraging-Based Model of Hunter-Gatherer Population Dynamics. Journal of Anthropological Archaeology,* 7, 329-372.

Berkes, F. (1986) *Common Property Resources and Hunting Territories* IN: Bishop, C. A. and Morantz, T., eds. *Who Owns the Beaver? Northern Algonkian Land Tenure Reconsidered.* Anthropological N.S. 28 (1-2), 145-162.

Bettinger, R. (1980) *Explanatory/Predictive Models of Hunter-Gather Adaptation* IN: Schiffer, M. B., ed. *Advances in Archaeological Method and Theory Vol. 3.* Academic Press, Toronto, pp. 189-255.

Bettinger, R. (1987) *Archaeological Approaches to Hunter-Gatherers. Annual Review of Anthropology,* 16, 121-142.

Bettinger, R. (1991) *Hunter-Gatherers: Archaeological and Evolutionary Theory.* Plenum Press, New York.

Binford, L. (1968a) *Methodological Considerations of the Archaeological Use of Ethnographic Data* IN: Lee, R. B. and Devore, I., eds. *Man the Hunter.* Aldine Publishing Company, Chicago, pp. 268-274.

Binford, S. R. (1968b) *Ethnographic Data and Understanding the Pleistocene* IN: Lee, R. B. and Devore, I., eds. *Man the Hunter.* Aldine Publishing Company, Chicago, pp. 274-275.

Bishop, C. A. (1970) *The emergence of hunting territories among the northern Ojibwa. Ethnology,* 9, 1-15.

Bishop, C. A. (1972) *Demography, Ecology and Trade Among the Northern Ojibwa and Swampy Cree. The Western Canadian Journal of Anthropology,* 3, 58-71.

Bishop, C. A. (1974) *The Northern Ojibwa and the Fur Trade: An Historical and Ecological Study.* Holt, Rinehart and Winston of Canada, Ltd., Toronto.

Bishop, C. A. (1981) *Indian Inhabitants of Northern Ontario at the Time of Contact: Socio-Territorial Considerations* IN: Hanna, M. G. and Kooyman, B., eds. *Approaches to Algonquian Archaeology: Proceedings of the Thirteenth Annual Conference.* The Archaeology Association of the University of Calgary, Calgary, pp. 253-273.

Bishop, C. A. (1986) *Territoriality Among Northeastern Algonquians* IN: Bishop, C. A. and Morantz, T., eds. *Who Owns the Beaver? Northern Algonkian Land Tenure Reconsidered.* Anthropological N.S. 28 (1-2), 37-63.

Brandt, R., Groenewoudt, B. J. and Kvamme, K. L. (1992) *An Experiment in archaeological site location: modeling in the Netherlands using GIS techniques. World Archaeology,* 24, 268-282.

Brody, H. (1988) *Maps and Dreams.* Douglas & McIntyre Ltd., Vancouver.

Broughton, J. M. (1994a) *Declines in mammalian foraging efficiency during the late Holocene, San Francisco Bay, California. Journal of Anthropological Archaeology,* 13, 371-401.

Broughton, J. M. (1994b) *Late Holocene resource intensification in the Sacramento Valley, California: the vertebrate evidence. Journal of Archaeological Science,* 21, 501-514.

Broughton, J. M. (1997) *Widening diet breadth, declining foraging efficiency, and prehistoric harvest pressure: ichthyofaunal evidence from the Emeryville Shellmound, California. Antiquity,* 71, 845-862.

Broughton, J. M. and O'Connell, J. F. (1999) *On Evolutionary Ecology, Selectionist Archaeology, and Behavioural Archaeology*. American Antiquity, 64, 163-165.

Brown, J. S. H. (1986) *Northern Algonkians from Lake Superior and Hudson Bay to Manitoba in the historical period* IN: Morrison, R. B. and Wilson, C. R., eds. *Native Peoples: The Canadian Experience*. McClelland and Stewart, Toronto, pp.

Brown, J. S. H. and Wilson, C. R. (1986) *The Northern Algonkians: A Regional Overview* IN: Morrison, R. B. and Wilson, C. R., eds. *Native Peoples: The Canadian Experience*. McClelland and Stewart, Toronto, pp. 143-149.

BRW Inc. (1996) *Research Design for the Development of a High Probability Predictive Model for Identifying Archaoelogical Sites*. Minneapolis, Minnesota Department of Transportation.

Buchner, A. P. (1979) *The 1978 Caribou Lake Project, including a summary of the prehistory of east-central Manitoba*. Dept. of Cultural Affairs & Historical Resources Historic Resources Branch, Winnipeg.

Buchner, A. P., Carmichael, P., Dickson, G., Dyck, I., Fardoe, B., Jones, T. L., Joyes, D., Mallory, O., Mallot, M., Meyer, D., Miller, D., Nash, R., Pettipas, L., Shay, C. T., Syms, E. L., Tisdale, M. A. and Whelan, J. P. (1983) *Introducing Manitoba prehistory*. Manitoba Dept. of Cultural Affairs and Historical Resources, Winnipeg.

Burrough, P. A. (1986) *Principles of GIS for Land Resources Assessment*. Clarendon Press, Oxford.

Carmichael, D. L. (1990) *GIS predictive modeling of prehistoric site distributions in central Montana* IN: Allen, K. M. S., Green, S. W. and Zubrow, E. B. W., eds. *Interpreting space: GIS and archaeology*. Taylor and Francis, London, pp. 216-225.

Cashdan, E. A. (1992) *Spatial Organization and Habitat Use* IN: Smith, E. A. and Winterhalder, B., eds. *Evolutionary Ecology and Human Behaviour*. Aldine De Gruyter, New York, pp. 237-266.

Chadwick, A. J. (1979) *Settlement Simulation* IN: Renfrew, C. and Cooke, K. L., eds. *Transformations: Mathematical Approaches to Culture Change*. Academic Press, New York, pp. 237-255.

Church, T., Brandon, R. J. and Burgett, G. R. (2000) *GIS Applications in Archaeology: Method in Search of Theory* IN: Wecott, K. L. and Brandon, R. J., eds. *Practical Applications of GIS for Archaeologists: A Predictive Modeling Kit*. Taylor and Francis, Philadelphia, pp. 135-155.

Clelland, C. E. (1966) *The Prehistoric Animal Ecology and Ethnology of the Upper Great Lakes Region*. Museum of Anthropology, University of Michigan, Ann Arbor.

Clelland, C. E. (1982) *The Inland Shore Fishery of the Northern Great Lakes: Its Development and Importance in Prehistory*. American Antiquity, 47, 761-784.

Cooper, J. M. (1939) *Is the Algonkian Family Hunting Ground System Pre-Columbian*. American Anthropologist, 41, 66-90.

Craik, B. and Casgrain, B. (1986) *Making a Living in the Bush: Land Tenure at Waskaganish* IN: Bishop, C. A. and Morantz, T., eds. *Who Owns the Beaver? Northern Algonkian Land Tenure Reconsidered*. Anthropological N.S. 28 (1-2), 175-186.

Dalla Bona, L. (1994a) *Cultural Heritage Resource Predictive Modeling Project: Vol. 3 Methodological Considerations*. Thunder Bay, ON., Centre For Archaeological Resource Prediction.

Dalla Bona, L. (1994b) *Cultural Heritage Resource Predictive Modeling Project: Vol. 4 A Predictive Model of Prehistoric Activity Location for Thunder Bay District, Ontario*. Center for Archaeological Resource Prediction, Thunder Bay.

Dalla Bona, L. and Larcombe, L. (1996) *Modeling Prehistoric Land Use in Northern Ontario* IN: Maschner, H. D. G., ed. *New Methods, Old Problems: Geographic Information Systems in Modern Archaeological Research*. Centre For Archaeological Investigation, Carbondale, Ill., pp. 252-271.

Damas, D. (1969) *Characteristics of Central Eskimo Band Structure* IN: Damas, D., ed. *Contributions to Anthropology: Band Societies*. National Museums of Canada, Ottawa, pp. 116-141.

Dawson, K. C. A. (1981) *The Northern Ojibwa of Ontario* IN: Hanna, M. G. and Kooyman, B., eds. *Approaches to Algonquian Archaeology: Proceedings of the Thirteenth Annual Conference*. The Archaeology Association of the University of Calgary, Calgary, pp. 81-96.

Dawson, K. C. A. (1983) *Prehistory of the Interior Forest of Northern Ontario* IN: Steegman, A. T., ed. *Boreal Forest Adaptations: The Northern Algonkians*. Plenum Press, New York, pp. 55-84.

De Boer, W. F. and Prins, H. H. T. (1989) *Decisions of Cattle Herdsmen in Burkina Faso and Optimal Foraging Models*. Human Ecology, 17, 445-464.

Dean, J. S., Gumerman, G. J., Epstein, J. M., Axtell, R. L., Swedlund, A. C., Parker, M. T. and McCarroll, S. (1999) *Understanding Anasazi Culture Change Through Agent-Based Modeling* IN: Kohler, T. and Gumerman, G., eds. *Dynamics in Human and Primate Societies*. Oxford University Press, New York, pp. 179-205.

Douglas, D. H. (1994) *Least-cost Path in GIS Using Accumulated Cost Surface and Slopelines*. Cartographica, 31, 37-51.

Duncan, R. B. and Beckman, K. A. (2000) *The Application of GIS Predictive Site Location*

Models within Pennsylvania and West Virginia IN: Wecott, K. L. and Brandon, R. J., eds. *Practical Applications of GIS for Archaeologists: A Predictive Modeling Kit.* Taylor and Francis, Philadelphia, pp. 33-58.

Dwyer, P. D. (1985) *A Hunt in New Guinea: Some Difficulties for Optimal Foraging Theory. Man (New Series),* 20, 243-253.

Ebert, J. I. (2000) *The State of the Art in "Inductive" Predictive Modeling: Seven Big Mistakes (and Lots of Smaller Ones)* IN: Wecott, K. L. and Brandon, R. J., eds. *Practical Applications of GIS for Archaeologists: A Predictive Modeling Kit.* Taylor and Francis, Philadelphia, pp. 129-134.

Feit, H. (1969) *Mistassini Hunters of the Boreal Forest Ecosystem Dynamics and Multiple Subsistence Patterns.* Master's Thesis, McGill University.

Feit, H. (1973) *The Ethno-Ecology of the Wasanipi Cree: or how hunters can manage their resources* IN: Cox, B., ed. *Cultural Ecology.* McClelland and Stewart, Toronto.

Fisher, A. D. (1969) *The Cree of Canada: Some Ecological and Evolutionary Considerations. Western Canadian Journal of Anthropology,* 1, 7-18.

Freeman Jr., L. G. (1968) *A Theoretical Framework for Interpreting Archaeological Materials* IN: Lee, R. B. and Devore, I., eds. *Man the Hunter.* Aldine Publishing Company, Chicago, pp. 262-267.

Gaffney, V. and van Leusen, P. M. (1995) *Postscript - GIS, environmental determinism and archaeology* IN: Lock, G. and Stancic, Z., eds. *Archaeology and Geographical Information Systems: A European Perspective.* Taylor and Francis, London, pp. 367-382.

Gardner, J. S. (1981) *General Environment* IN: Helm, J., ed. *Handbook of North American Indians: Subarctic.* Smithsonian Institution, Washington, D. C., pp. 5-14.

Gilbert, N. (1999) *Modeling Sociality: The View from Europe* IN: Kohler, T. and Gumerman, G., eds. *Dynamics in Human and Primate Societies.* Oxford University Press, New York, pp. 355-371.

Gillespie, B. C. (1981) *Major Fauna in the Traditional Economy* IN: Helm, J., ed. *Handbook of North American Indians: Subarctic.* Smithsonian Institution, Washington, D. C., pp. 15-18.

Hallowell, A. I. (1992) *The Ojibwa of Berens River, Manitoba: Ethnography into History.* Harcourt Brace Jovanovich College Publishers, Toronto.

Hamilton, S. (2000) *Archaeological Predictive Modeling in the Boreal Forest: No Easy Answers. Canadian Journal of Archaeology,* 24, 41-76.

Hamilton, S., Dalla Bona, L. and Larcombe, L. (1994) *Cultural Heritage Resource Predictive Modeling Project: Volume 5 Summary and Recommendations.* Center for Archaeological Resource Prediction, Thunder Bay.

Hamilton, S. and Larcombe, L. (1994) *Cultural Heritage Resource Predictive Modeling Project: Volume 1 Introduction to the Research.* Center for Archaeological Resource Prediction, Thunder Bay.

Harris, T. (2000) *Session 2 discussion: Moving GIS: movement within prehistoric cultural landscapes using GIS* IN: Lock, G., ed. *Beyond the Map: Archaeology and Spatial Technologies.* IOS Press, Amsterdam, pp. 116-123.

Hasenstab, R. J. (1996) *Settlement as Adaptation: Variability in Iroquois Village Site Selection As Inferred Through GIS* IN: Maschner, H. D. G., ed. *New Methods, Old Problems: Geographic Information Systems in Modern Archaeological Research.* Centre For Archaeological Investigation, Carbondale, Ill., pp. 223-241.

Hawkes, K., Hill, K. and O'Connell, J. F. (1982) *Why Hunters Gather: Optimal Foraging and the Ache of Eastern Paraguay. American Ethnologist,* 9, 379-398.

Hawkes, K. and O'Connell, J. (1992) *On Optimal Foraging Models and Subsistence Transitions. Current Anthropology,* 33, 63-66.

Hickerson, H. (1988) *The Chippewa and their Neighbours: A Study in Ethnohistory.* Holt, Rinehart and Winston, New York.

Hill, K. (1988) *Macronutrient Modifications of Optimal Foraging Theory: An Approach Using Indifference Curves Applied to Some Modern Foragers. Human Ecology,* 16, 157-197.

Jochim, M. (1979) *Breaking Down the System: Recent Ecological Approaches in Archaeology* IN: Schiffer, M. B., ed. *Advances in Archaeological Method and Theory.* Academic Press, Toronto, pp. 77-117.

Jochim, M. (1983) *Optimization Models in Context* IN: Moore, J. A. and Keene, A. S., eds. *Archaeological Hammers and Theories.* Academic Press, Toronto, pp. 157-172.

Jochim, M. (1988) *Optimal Foraging and the Division of Labour. American Anthropologist,* 90, 130-136.

Judge, W. J. and Sebastian, L. (1988) *Quantifying the present and predicting the past: theory, method, and application of archaeological predictive modeling.* U.S. Department of the Interior, Bureau of Land Management, Denver.

Kamermans, H. and Wansleeben, M. (1999) *Predictive Modeling in Dutch Archaeology, Joining Forces* IN: Barcelo, J. A., Briz, I. and Vila, A., eds. *New Techniques for Old Times: Computer Applications and Quantitative Methods in Archaeology.* BAR Publishing, Oxford, pp. 225-229.

Kaplan, H. and Hill, K. (1992) *The Evolutionary Ecology of Food Acquisition* IN: Smith, E. A. and Winterhalder, B., eds. *Evolutionary Ecology and Human Behaviour.* Aldine De Gruyter, New York, pp. 167-201.

Keegan, W. F. (1986) *The Optimal Foraging Analysis of Horticultural Production*. American Anthropologist, 87, 92-107.

Keene, A. S. (1979) *Economic Optimization Models and the Study of Hunter-Gatherer Subsistence Settlement Systems* IN: Renfrew, C. and Cooke, K. L., eds. *Transformations: Mathematical Approaches to Culture Change.* Academic Press, New York, pp. 369-404.

Keene, A. S. (1981) *Prehistoric Foraging in a Temperate Forest: A Linear Programming Example.* Academic Press, New York.

Keene, A. S. (1983) *Biology, Behaviour and Borrowing: A Critical Examination of Optimal Foraging Theory in Archaeology* IN: Moore, J. A. and Keene, A. S., eds. *Archaeological Hammers and Theories.* Academic Press, Toronto, pp. 137-155.

Kincaid, C. (1988) *Predictive Modeling and its Relationship to Cultural Resource Management Applications* IN: Judge, W. J. and Sebastian, L., eds. *Quantifying the present and predicting the past: Theory, method and application of archaeological predictive modeling.* Government Printing Office, Washington, D. C., pp. 549-569.

Kohler, T. A. (1988) *Predictive Locational Modeling: History and Current Practice* IN: Judge, W. J. and Sebastian, L., eds. *Quantifying the present and predicting the past: Theory, method and application of archaeological predictive modeling.* Government Printing Office, Washington, D. C., pp. 19-59.

Kohler, T. A. (1999) *Putting Social Sciences Together Again: An Introduction to the Volume* IN: Kohler, T. and Gumerman, G., eds. *Dynamics in Human and Primate Societies.* Oxford University Press, New York, pp. 1-18.

Kohler, T. A., Kresl, J., van West, C., Carr, E. and Wilshusen, R. H. (1999) *Be There Then: A Modeling Approach to Settlement Determinants and Spatial Efficiency Among Late Ancestral Pueblo Populations of the Mesa Verde Region, U.S. Southwest* IN: Kohler, T. and Gumerman, G., eds. *Dynamics in Human and Primate Societies.* Oxford University Press, New York, pp. 145-178.

Kohler, T. A. and Parker, S. C. (1986) *Predictive Models for Archaeological Resource Location* IN: Schiffer, M. B., ed. *Advances in Archaeological Method and Theory Vol. 9.* Academic Press, Toronto, pp. 397-452.

Krist, F. J. and Brown, D. G. (1994) *GIS Modeling of Paleo-Indian Period Caribou Migrations and Viewsheds in Northeastern Lower Michigan.* Photogrammetric Engineering and Remote Sensing, 60, 1129-1137.

Kuna, M. and Adelsbergerova, D. (1995) *Prehistoric location preferences: an application of GIS to the Vinorsky-potok project, Bohemia, the Czech Republic* IN: Lock, G. and Stancic, Z., eds. *Archaeology and Geographical Information Systems: A European Perspective.* Taylor and Francis, London, pp. 117-132.

Kurland, J. A. and Beckerman, S. J. (1985) *Optimal Foraging and Hominid Evolution: Labor and Reciprocity.* American Anthropologist, 87, 73-93.

Kvamme, K. L. (1985) *Determining Empirical Relationships Between the Natural Environment and Prehistoric Site Locations* IN: Carr, C., ed. *For Concordance in Archaeological Analysis: Bridging Data Structure, Quantitative Technique and Theory.* Westport Publishers Inc, Kansas City, MO, pp. 208-238.

Kvamme, K. L. (1988a) *Development and Testing of Quantitative Models* IN: Judge, W. J. and Sebastian, L., eds. *Quantifying the present and predicting the past: Theory, method and application of archaeological predictive modeling.* Government Printing Office, Washington, D. C., pp. 325-348.

Kvamme, K. L. (1988b) *Using Existing Archaeological Survey Data for Model Building* IN: Judge, W. J. and Sebastian, L., eds. *Quantifying the present and predicting the past: Theory, method and application of archaeological predictive modeling.* Government Printing Office, Washington, D. C., pp. 301-323.

Kvamme, K. L. (1990) *One-Sample Tests in Regional Archaeological Analysis: New Possibilities Through Computer Technology.* American Antiquity, 55, 367-381.

Kvamme, K. L. (1992) *A Predictive Site Location Model on the High Plains: An Example with an Independent Test.* Plains Anthropologist, 37, 19-40.

Kvamme, K. L. and Jochim, M. A. (1989) *The Environmental Basis of Mesolithic Settlement* IN: Bonsall, C., ed. *The Mesolithic in Europe: Papers Presented at the Third International Symposium, Edinburgh 1985.* John Donald Publishers Ltd., Edinburgh, pp. 1-12.

Lake, M. W. (1999) *MAGICAL Computer Simulation of Mesolithic Foraging* IN: Kohler, T. and Gumerman, G., eds. *Dynamics in Human and Primate Societies.* Oxford University Press, New York, pp. 107-143.

Larcombe, L. (1994) *Cultural Heritage Reource Predictive Modeling Project: Volume 2 Boreal Forest Aboriginal Land Use Patterns: An Evaluation of the Ethnographic Literature.* Center for Archaeological Resource Prediction, Thunder Bay.

Leacock, E. (1969) *The Montagnais-Naskapi Band* IN: Damas, D., ed. *Contributions to Anthropology: Band Societies.* National Museums of Canada, Ottawa, pp. 1-20.

Lenius, B. J. and Olinyk, D. M. (1990) *The Rainy River Composite: Revisions to Late Woodland Taxonomy* IN: Gibbon, G. E., ed. *The Woodland Tradition in the Western Great Lakes: Papers*

Presented to Elden Johnson. University of Minnesota Publications in Anthropology, Minneapolis, pp. 77-112.

Llobera, M. (2000) *Understanding movement: a pilot model towards the sociology of movement* IN: Lock, G., ed. *Beyond the Map: Archaeology and Spatial Technologies*. IOS Press, Amsterdam, pp. 65-84.

Malasiuk, J. A. (1999) *Aboriginal Land Use Patterns in the Boreal Forest of North-Central Manitoba: Applications for Archaeology*. Masters, University of Manitoba.

Manitoba Model Forest Inc. (1999) *Manitoba Model Forest Annual Report, 1998/98*. Natural Resources Canada, Ottawa.

Marles, R. J., Clavelle, C., Monteleone, L., Tays, N. and Burns, D. (2000) *Aboriginal Plant Use in Canada's Northwest Boreal Forest*. UBC Press, Vancouver.

Marozas, B. A. and Zack, J. A. (1990) *GIS and archaeological site location* IN: Allen, K. M. S., Green, S. W. and Zubrow, E. B. W., eds. *Interpreting space: GIS and archaeology*. Taylor and Francis, London, pp. 165-172.

Martijn, C. A. and Rogers, E. S. (1969) *Mistassini-Albanel: Contributions to the Prehistory of Quebec*. Université Laval, Quebec.

Martin, J. F. (1983) *Optimal Foraging Theory: A Review of Some Models and Their Applications*. American Anthropologist, 85, 612-629.

Martin, J. F. (1985) *More on Optimal Foraging Theory*. American Anthropologist, 87, 649-650.

Maschner, H. (1996) *The Politics of Settlement Choice on the Northwest Coast: Cognition, GIS and Coastal Landscapes* IN: Maschner, H. D. G., ed. *New Methods, Old Problems: Geographic Information Systems in Modern Archaeological Problems*. Southern Illinois University, Carbondale, IL, pp. 175-189.

McArthur, R. H. and Pianka, E. R. (1966) *On optimal use of a patchy environment. American Naturalist*, 100, 603-609.

McKennan, R. A. (1969) *Athapaskan Groupings and Social Organization In Central Alaska* IN: Damas, D., ed. *Contributions to Anthropology: Band Societies*. National Museums of Canada, Ottawa, pp. 93-115.

Menard, S. (1995) *Applied Logistic Regression Analysis*. Sage Publications, Thousand Oaks, CA.

Meyer, D. and Hamilton, S. (1994) *Neighbors to the North: Peoples of the Boreal Forest* IN: Schlesier, K. H., ed. *Plains Indians, A.D. 500-1500: The Archaeological Past of Historic Groups*. University of Oklahoma Press, Norman, pp. 96-127.

Mithen, S. J. (1989) *Modeling Hunter-Gatherer Decision Making: Complementing Optimal Foraging Theory. Human Ecology*, 17, 59-83.

Palidwor, K. L. and Schindler, D. W. (1995) *Habitat Suitability Index Models Within the Manitoba Model Forest Area: Woodland Caribou*. Pine Falls, Manitoba Model Forest Inc.

Palidwor, K. L., Schindler, D. W. and Hagglund, B. R. (1995) *Habitat Suitability Index Models Within the Manitoba Model Forest Region: Moose (Version 2.0)*. Pine Falls, Manitoba Model Forest.

Parker, S. (1985) *Predictive Modeling of Site Settlement Systems Using Multivariate Logistics* IN: Carr, C., ed. *For Concordance in Archaeological Analysis: Bridging Data Structure, Quantitative Technique and Theory*. Westport Publishers, Inc., Kansas City, MO, pp. 173-207.

Petch, V. and Larcombe, L. (1998) *Manitoba Model Forest Archaeological and Anishinabe Pimadaziwin Data Base Project*. Pine Falls, MB., Manitoba Model Forest Inc.

Petch, V., Larcombe, L., Pettipas, L., Ebert, D. and Senior, G. (2000) *Manitoba Model Forest Predictive Modeling For Archaeological Site Location*. Pine Falls, MB., Manitoba Model Forest Inc.

Ray, A. S. (1974) *Indians in the Fur Trade*. University of Toronto Press, Toronto.

Reynolds, R. G. (1999) *The Impact of Raiding on Settlement Patterns in the Northern Valley of Oaxaca: An Approach Using Decision Trees* IN: Kohler, T. and Gumerman, G., eds. *Dynamics in Human and Primate Societies*. Oxford University Press, New York, pp. 251-273.

Rogers, E. S. (1962) *The Round Lake Ojibwa*. Art and Archaeology Division, Royal Ontario Museum, Toronto.

Rogers, E. S. (1963a) *Changing Settlement Patterns of the Cree-Ojibwa of Northern Ontario. Southwestern Journal of Anthropology*, 64-88.

Rogers, E. S. (1963b) *The Hunting Group-Hunting Territory Complex Among the Mistassi Indians*. National Museums of Canada, Ottawa.

Rogers, E. S. (1963c) *The Material Culture of the Mistassini*. National Museums of Canada, Ottawa.

Rogers, E. S. (1969) *Band Organization Among the Indians of Eastern Subarctic Canada* IN: Damas, D., ed. *Contributions to Anthropology: Band Societies*. National Museums of Canada, Ottawa, pp. 21-55.

Rogers, E. S. (1986) *Epilogue: Reevaluations and Future Considerations* IN: Bishop, C. A. and Morantz, T., eds. *Who Owns the Beaver? Northern Algonkian Land Tenure Reconsidered*. Anthropological N.S. 28 (1-2), 203-216.

Rose, M. R. and Altschul, J. H. (1988) *An Overview of Statistical Method and Theory for Quantitative Model Building* IN: Judge, W. J. and Sebastian, L., eds. *Quantifying the present and predicting the past: Theory, method and application of archaeological predictive modeling*. Government Printing Office, Washington, D. C., pp. 173-255.

Ruggles, A. J. and Church, R. L. (1996) *An Analysis of Late-Horizon Settlement Patterns in the Teotihuacan-Temascalapa Basins: A Location-Allocation and GIS-Based Approach* IN: Maschner, H. D. G., ed. *New Methods, Old Problems: Geographic Information Systems in Modern Archaeological Problems.* Southern Illinois University, Carbondale, IL, pp. 155-174.

Saylor, S. (1989) *EgKx-1, Wanipigow: Introduction and Background. Manitoba Archaeological Quarterly,* 13, 1-27.

Schrire, C. (1984) *Wild Surmises on Savage Thoughts* IN: Schrire, C., ed. *Past and Present in Hunter-Gatherer Studies.* Academic Press, Toronto, pp. 1-25.

Schwimmer, B., Petch, V. and Larcombe, L. (2002) *Manitoba Heritage Network.* [Internet] Available from: http://www.umanitoba.ca/faculties/arts/anthropology/manarchnet/toc.html [April].

Scott, G. A. J. (1995) *Canada's Vegetation: A World Perspective.* McGill-Queen's University Press, Montreal & Kingston.

Sebastian, L. and Judge, W. J. (1988) *Predicting the Past: Correlation, Explanation and the Use of Archaeological Models* IN: Judge, W. J. and Sebastian, L., eds. *Quantifying the present and predicting the past: Theory, method and application of archaeological predictive modeling.* Government Printing Office, Washington, D. C., pp. 1-18.

Sieciechowicz, K. (1986) *Northern Ojibwa Land Tenure* IN: Bishop, C. A. and Morantz, T., eds. *Who Owns the Beaver? Northern Algonkian Land Tenure Reconsidered.* Anthropological N.S. 28 (1-2), 187-200.

Simpson, L. (1999) *The construction of traditional ecological knowledge: issues, implications and insights.* PhD, University of Manitoba.

Smith, E. A. (1983) *Anthropological Applications of Optimal Foraging Theory: A Critical Review. Current Anthropology,* 24, 625-651.

Smith, E. A. (1988) *Risk and uncertainty in the 'original affluent society': evolutionary ecology of resource-sharing and land tenure* IN: Ingold, T., Riches, D. and Woodburn, J., eds. *Hunters and Gatherers 1: History, evolution and social change.* Berg, Oxford, pp. 222-251.

Smith, E. A. (1991) *Inujjuamiut Foraging Strategies.* Aldine De Gruyter, New York.

Smith, J. G. E. (1981) *Western Woods Cree* IN: Helm, J., ed. *Handbook of North American Indians: Vol.6 Subarctic.* Smithsonian Institution, Washington, D.C., pp. 256-270.

Speck, F. (1915) *The family hunting band as the basis of Algonkian Social Organization. American Anthropologist,* 17, 289-305.

Speck, F. (1973) *The Family Hunting Band as the basis of Algonkian Social Organization* IN: Cox, B., ed. *Cultural Ecology.* McClelland and Stewart, Toronto, pp. 58-75.

Stancic, Z. and Kvamme, K. L. (1999) *Settlement Pattern Modelling through Boolean Overlays of Social and Environmental Variables* IN: Barcelo, J. A., Briz, I. and Vila, A., eds. *New Techniques for Old Times: Computer Applications and Quantitative Methods in Archaeology.* BAR Publishing, Oxford, pp. 231-237.

Steegman, A. T. (1983a) *Boreal Forest Hazards and Adaptations: The Past* IN: Steegman, A. T., ed. *Boreal Forest Adaptations: The Northern Algonkians.* Plenum Press, New York, pp. 243-267.

Steegman, A. T. (1983b) *The Northern Algonkian Project and Changing Perceptions of Human Adaptation* IN: Steegman, A. T., ed. *Boreal Forest Adaptations: The Northern Algonkians.* Plenum Press, New York, pp. 1-8.

Steegman, A. T., Hurlich, M. G. and Winterhalder, B. (1983) *Coping with Cold and Other Challenges of the Boreal Forest: An Overview* IN: Steegman, A. T., ed. *Boreal Forest Adaptations: The Northern Algonkians.* Plenum Press, New York, pp. 317-351.

Stein Mandryk, C. A. (1993) *Hunter-Gatherer Social Costs and the Nonviability of Submarginal Environments. Journal of Anthropological Research,* 49, 39-71.

Steinbring, J. (1981) *Saulteaux of Lake Winnipeg* IN: Helm, J., ed. *Handbook of North American Indians: Vol.6 Subarctic.* Smithsonian Institution, Washington, D.C., pp. 244-255.

Tanner, A. (1973) *The Significance of Hunting Territories Today* IN: Cox, B., ed. *Cultural Ecology.* McClelland and Stewart, Toronto, pp. 101-114.

Tanner, A. (1979) *Bringing Home Animals: Religious Ideology and Mode of Production.* Institute of Social and Economic Research, Memorial University, St John.

Tanner, A. (1986) *The New Hunting Territory Debate: An Introduction to Some Unresolved Issues* IN: Bishop, C. A. and Morantz, T., eds. *Who Owns the Beaver? Northern Algonkian Land Tenure Reconsidered.* Anthropological N.S. 28 (1-2), 19-36.

van Leusen, P. M. (1999) *Viewshed and Cost Surface Anlysis Using GIS (Cartographic Modelling in a Cell-Based GIS II)* IN: Barcelo, J. A., Briz, I. and Vila, A., eds. *New Techniques for Old Times: Computer Applications and Quantitative Methods in Archaeology.* BAR Publishing, Oxford, pp. 215-223.

Van West, C. (1994) *Modeling Prehistoric Agricultural Productivity in Southwestern Colorado: A GIS Approach.* Washington State University, Pullman.

Warren, R. E. (1990a) *Predictive modeling in archaeology: a primer* IN: Allen, K. M. S., Green, S. W. and Zubrow, E. B. W., eds. *Interpreting space: GIS and archaeology.* Taylor and Francis, London, pp. 90-111.

Warren, R. E. (1990b) *Predictive modeling of archaeological site location: a case study in the Midwest* IN: Allen, K. M. S., Green, S. W. and Zubrow, E. B. W., eds. *Interpreting space: GIS and archaeology.* Taylor and Francis, London, pp. 201-215.

Warren, R. E. and Asch, D. L. (2000) *A Predictive Model of Archaeological Site Location in the Eastern Prairie Peninsula* IN: Wescott, K. L. and Brandon, R. J., eds. *Practical Applications of GIS for Archaeologists: A Predictive Modeling Kit.* Taylor and Francis, Philadelphia, pp. 5-32.

Weimer, M. B. (1995) *Predictive Modeling and Cultural Resource Management: An Alternative View from the Plains Periphery* IN: Duke, P. and Wilson, M. C., eds. *Beyond Subsistence: Plains Archaeology and the Postprocessual Critique.* The University of Alabama Press, Tuscaloosa, AL, pp. 90-109.

Wheatley, D. W. (1993) *Going over old ground: GIS, archaeological theory and the act of perception* IN: Andresen, J., Scollar, I. and Madsen, T., eds. *Computing the Past: Computing Applications and Quantitative Methods in Archaeology CAA92.* Aarhus University Press, Aarhus, pp. 133-138.

Wheatley, D. W. (1996) *Between the lines: the role of GIS-based predictive modelling in the interpretation of extensive survey data* IN: Kamermans, H. and Fennema, K., eds. *Interfacing the Past: Computer Applications and Quantitative Methods in Archaeology CAA95.* Analecta Praehistoica Leidensia, Leiden, pp.

Winterhalder, B. P. (1977) *Foraging Strategy Adaptations of the Boreal Forest Cree: An Evaluation of Theory and Models from Evolutionary Ecology.* Doctoral thesis, Cornell University.

Winterhalder, B. P. (1981a) *Foraging Strategies in the Boreal Forest: An Analysis of Cree Hunting and Gathering* IN: Winterhalder, B. and Smith, E. A., eds. *Hunter-Gatherer Foraging Strategies: Ethnographic and Archaeological Analyses.* University of Chicago Press, Chicago, pp. 66-98.

Winterhalder, B. P. (1981b) *Optimal Foraging Strategies and Hunter-Gatherer Research in Anthropology: Theory and Models* IN: Winterhalder, B. and Smith, E. A., eds. *Hunter-Gatherer Foraging Strategies: Ethnographic and Archaeological Analyses.* University of Chicago Press, Chicago, pp. 13-35.

Winterhalder, B. P. (1983) *History and Ecology of the Boreal Zone in Ontario* IN: Steegman, A. T., ed. *Boreal Forest Adaptations: The Northern Algonkians.* Plenum Press, New York, pp. 9-54.

Winterhalder, B. P. (1994) *Concept in Historical Ecology: The View from Evolutionary Ecology* IN: Crumley, C. L., ed. *Historical Ecology: Cultural Knowledge and Changing Landscapes.* School of American Research Press, Santa Fe, NM, pp. 17-41.

Winterhalder, B. P., Baillargeon, W., Cappelletto, F., Daniel, I. R. and Prescott, C. (1988) *The Population Ecology of Hunter-Gatherers and Their Prey. Journal of Anthropological Archaeology,* 7, 289-328.

Yesner, D. R. (1985) *Archaeology and Optimal Foraging Theory: Appropriate Analytical Units. American Anthropologist,* 87, 412-414.

Zutter, C. (1989) *Predicting North American Late Pleistocene Archaeology Using an Optimal Foraging Model. Canadian Journal of Archaeology,* 13, 69-96.

Appendix 1: Site Database

Table 26: Borden Numbers of Woodland Sites in the Study Area

EfKv-1	EfKv-12	EfKv-14
EfKv-15	EfKv-16	EfKv-19
EfKv-2	EfKv-20	EfKv-21
EfKv-22	EfKv-23	EfKv-25
EfKv-26	EfKv-27	EfKv-28
EfKv-29	EfKv-3	EfKv-30
EfKv-31	EfKv-33	EfKv-34
EfKv-35	EfKv-36	EfKv-38
EfKv-39	EfKv-40	EfKv-41
EfKv-42	EfKv-43	EfKv-44
EfKv-45	EfKv-46	EfKv-47
EfKv-48	EfKv-49	EfKv-5
EfKv-50	EfKv-51	EfKv-52
EfKv-55	EfKv-56	EfKv-57
EfKv-58	EfKv-59	EfKv-6
EfKv-60	EfKv-61	EfKv-62
EfKv-64	EfKv-65	EfKv-7
EfKv-9	EfKw-1	EfKw-2
EfKw-3	EgKx-1	EgKx-11
EgKx-12	EgKx-14	EgKx-15
EgKx-16	EgKx-7	EgKx-18
EgKx-19	EgKx-2	EgKx-20
EgKx-5	EgKx-6	EgKx-7
EgKx-8	EgLa-1	EgLa-10
EgLa-13	EgLa-2	EgLa-3
EgLa-4	EgLa-5	EgLa-6
EgLa-7	EgLa-8	EgLa-9

Table 27: Survey 2000 Site Discoveries

Borden Number	Site Name	Cultural Affiliation
EgKw-8	Rusty Tin Cans	Historic
EgKw-9	Sawed Bone	Historic
EfKw-9	Yankee Girl	Precontact
No Number	Mine	Historic
EgKw-10	Marker	Undated
EgKw-3	Recon Quarry	Undated
EgKw-4	Recon II	Undated
EgKw-14	Stabbed Leg	Undated
EgKw-2	JarJar Binks	Precontact
EgKw-13	Whee Rapids	Undated
EgKw-12	Blair Witch	Undated
EgKw-17	Pirate Hill	Undated
EgKw-15	Pee-Oh-Ed	Undated
EgKw-16	MI2	Undated
EgKw-5	Thunderbird Nest	Undated
EgKw-3	M2	Undated
EgKw-7	P.B.	Undated
EgKw-11	Scream	Undated
EgKv-4	Tins Galore	Historic
EgKw-18	Everquest	Undated
EgKw-19	Hot Rocks	Undated

Table 28: Survey 2001 Site Discoveries

Borden Number	Site Name	Cultural Affiliation
EiLc-2	Rice River 2	None Assigned
EiLc-3	Rice River 1	Middle & Late Precontact
EiLc-5	Rice River Alone	Woodland
EiLc-6	Kakeeskapechewunk Rapids	Middle & Late Precontact
EiLc-7	Rice River Settlement	Late Precontact, Historic
EiLc-8	Popular Point Island	Late Precontact
EiLc-9	Rice River Fork	Late Precontact
EiLb-1	Rice River Pictograph	Undated
EiLb-2	Stolen Site	Late Precontact
EiLb-3	Made in the Shade	Middle & Late Precontact; Historic
EiLb-4	Shallow Lake Trapper's Cabin	Recent Historic
EiLb-5	Tree Throw	Late Precontact
EiLb-6	Bird	Late Precontact
EiLb-7	Shallow Lake Petroform	Late Precontact
EiLb-8	Shallow Lake Old Settlement	Late Precontact
EiLb-9	Swim	Late Precontact
EiLb-10	Raven's Cabin	Late Precontact
EiLb-11	Lodge	Recent Historic
EiLc-1	Rice River Settlement Cemetery	Late Precontact; Middle to Late Historic
EiLc-10	Rice Point	Late Precontact; Early Historic
EiLc-11	Hamilton Beach	Late Precontact; Late Historic
EiLc-12	Sandy Veal Beach	Late Precontact; Early to Middle Historic

Appendix 2: Variable Statistical Testing

1.0 Cultural Variables Statistical Testing

1.1 Distance to Ceremonial Resources Statistical Testing

H_0 – There is no difference between the distribution of sites in relation distance to ceremonial resources and the general distribution of cells in the environment and their distance to ceremonial resources

H_a – There is a difference between the distribution of sites in relation to distance to ceremonial resources and the general distribution of cells in the environment and their distance to ceremonial resources

Table 29: Distance to Ceremonial Resources Statistical Testing

Distance to Ceremonial Resources	Sites	Cumulative Percent	Cells in the Environment	Cumulative Percent	Difference
0-3000m	0	0.000	40738	0.017	-0.017
3001-6000m	0	0.000	91532	0.057	-0.057
6000-9000m	0	0.000	71395	0.087	-0.087
9000m+	81	1.000	2124735	1.000	0.000

Dmax = 0.087 – therefore accept the H_0 and state that there is no significant difference in site location. In other words, sites are distributed randomly in relation to the distance to ceremonial resources.

1.2 Distance to Earth Resources Statistical Testing

H_0 – There is no difference between the distribution of sites in relation distance to earth resources and the general distribution of cells in the environment and their distance to earth resources

H_a – There is a difference between the distribution of sites in relation to distance to earth resources and the general distribution of cells in the environment and their distance to earth resources

Table 30: Distance to Earth Resources Statistical Testing

Distance to Earth Resources	Sites	Cumulative Percent	Cells in the Environment	Cumulative Percent	Difference
0-3000m	66	0.815	355589	0.153	0.662
3001-6000m	15	1.000	606918	0.413	0.587
6000-9000m	0	1.000	495920	0.626	0.374
9000m+	0	1.000	869973	1.000	0.000

Dmax = 0.662 – therefore reject the H_0 and state that there is a significant difference in site location. In other words, sites are distributed non-randomly in relation to the distance to earth resources.

1.3 Distance to Faunal Resources Statistical Testing

H_0 – There is no difference between the distribution of sites in relation distance to faunal resources and the general distribution of cells in the environment and their distance to faunal resources

H_a – There is a difference between the distribution of sites in relation to distance to faunal resources and the general distribution of cells in the environment and their distance to faunal resources

Table 31: Distance to Faunal Resources Statistical Testing

Distance to Faunal Resources	Sites	Cumulative Percent	Cells in the Environment	Cumulative Percent	Difference
0-3000m	9	0.111	55599	0.024	0.087
3001-6000m	22	0.383	90814	0.063	0.320
6000-9000m	12	0.531	106746	0.109	0.422
9000m+	38	1.000	2075241	1.000	0.000

Dmax = 0.422 – therefore reject the H_0 and state that there is a significant difference in site location. In other words, sites are distributed non-randomly in relation to the distance to faunal resources.

1.4 Distance to Industrial Resources Statistical Testing

H_0 – There is no difference between the distribution of sites in relation distance to industrial resources and the general distribution of cells in the environment and their distance to industrial resources

H_a – There is a difference between the distribution of sites in relation to distance to industrial resources and the general distribution of cells in the environment and their distance to industrial resources

Table 32: Distance to Industrial Resources Statistical Testing

Distance to Industrial Resources	Sites	Cumulative Percent	Cells in the Environment	Cumulative Percent	Difference
0-3000m	26	0.321	123906	0.053	0.268
3001-6000m	20	0.568	345426	0.202	0.366
6000-9000m	16	0.765	417905	0.381	0.384
9000m+	19	1.000	1441163	1.000	0.000

Dmax = 0.384 – therefore reject the H_0 and state that there is a significant difference in site location. In other words, sites are distributed non-randomly in relation to the distance to industrial resources.

1.5 Distance to Local Resources Statistical Testing

H_0 – There is no difference between the distribution of sites in relation distance to local resources and the general distribution of cells in the environment and their distance to local resources

H_a – There is a difference between the distribution of sites in relation to distance to local resources and the general distribution of cells in the environment and their distance to local resources

Table 33: Distance to Local Resources Statistical Testing

Distance to Local Resources	Sites	Cumulative Percent	Cells in the Environment	Cumulative Percent	Difference
0-3000m	13	0.160	172505	0.074	0.086
3001-6000m	13	0.321	408548	0.250	0.071
6000-9000m	5	0.383	543181	0.483	-0.100
9000m+	50	1.000	1204166	1.000	0.000

Dmax = 0.086 – therefore accept the H_0 and state that there is no significant difference in site location. In other words, sites are distributed randomly in relation to the distance to local resources.

1.6 Distance to Trails and Cabins Statistical Testing

H_0 – There is no difference between the distribution of sites in relation distance to trails and cabins and the general distribution of cells in the environment and their distance to trails and cabins

H_a – There is a difference between the distribution of sites in relation to distance to trails and cabins and the general distribution of cells in the environment and their distance to trails and cabins

Table 34: Distance to Local Resources Statistical Testing

Distance to Trails and Cabins	Sites	Cumulative Percent	Cells in the Environment	Cumulative Percent	Difference
0-3000m	13	0.160	152818	0.066	0.095
3001-6000m	33	0.568	248047	0.172	0.396
6000-9000m	9	0.679	276934	0.291	0.388
9000m+	26	1.000	1650601	1.000	0.000

Dmax = 0.388 – therefore reject the H_0 and state that there is a significant difference in site location. In other words, sites are distributed non-randomly in relation to the distance to trails and cabins.

1.7 Distance to Vegetative Resources Statistical Testing

H_0 – There is no difference between the distribution of sites in relation distance to vegetative resources and the general distribution of cells in the environment and their distance vegetative resources

H_a – There is a difference between the distribution of sites in relation to distance to vegetative resources and the general distribution of cells in the environment and their distance to vegetative resources

Table 35: Distance to Vegetative Resources Statistical Testing

Distance to Vegetative Resources	Sites	Cumulative Percent	Cells in the Environment	Cumulative Percent	Difference
0-3000m	53	0.654	391828	0.168	0.486
3001-6000m	25	0.963	598830	0.425	0.537
6000-9000m	3	1.000	547777	0.661	0.339
9000m+	0	1.000	789965	1.000	0.000

Dmax = 0.537 – therefore reject the H_0 and state that there is a significant difference in site location. In other words, sites are distributed non-randomly in relation to the distance to vegetative resources.

2.0 Economic Variable Statistical Testing

2.1 Moose Habitat Suitability Index Statistical Testing

H_0 – There is no difference between the distribution of sites in relation to the moose habitat suitability index and the general distribution of cells in the environment and their moose habitat suitability index

H_a – There is a difference between the distribution of sites in relation to the moose habitat suitability index and the general distribution of cells in the environment and their moose habitat suitability index

Table 36: Moose Habitat Suitability Index Statistical Testing

Moose Habitat Suitability Index	Sites	Cumulative Percent	Cells in the Environment	Cumulative Percent	Difference
0-0.33	67	0.827	2202852	0.950	-0.123
0.34-0.66	14	1.00	115172	1.000	0.000
0.67-1	0	1.00	0	1.000	0.000

Dmax = 0.123 – therefore accept the H_0 and state that there is no significant difference in site location. In other words, sites are distributed randomly in relation to the moose habitat suitability index.

2.2 Woodland Caribou Habitat Suitability Index Statistical Testing

H_0 – There is no difference between the distribution of sites in relation to the woodland caribou habitat suitability index and the general distribution of cells in the environment and their woodland caribou habitat suitability index

H_a – There is a difference between the distribution of sites in relation to the woodland caribou habitat suitability index and the general distribution of cells in the environment and their woodland caribou habitat suitability index

Table 37: Woodland Caribou Habitat Suitability Index Statistical Testing

Woodland Caribou Habitat Suitability Index	Sites	Cumulative Percent	Cells in the Environment	Cumulative Percent	Difference
0-0.33	62	0.765	1155552	0.530	0.235
0.34-0.66	0	0.765	175828	0.611	0.155
0.67-1	19	1.000	848249	1.000	0.000

Dmax = 0.235 – therefore reject the H_0 and state that there is a significant difference in site location. In other words, sites are distributed randomly in relation to the woodland caribou habitat suitability index.

3.0 Environmental Variables Statistical Testing

3.1 Aspect Statistical Testing

H_0 – There is no difference between the distribution of sites in relation aspect and the general distribution of cells in the environment and their aspect
H_a – There is a difference between the distribution of sites in relation to aspect and the general distribution of cells in the environment and their aspect

Table 38: Aspect Statistical Testing

Aspect Class	Sites	Cumulative Percent	Cells in the Environment	Cumulative Percent	Difference
Flat	11	0.136	111100	0.048	0.088
North	4	0.185	295275	0.175	0.011
Northeast	10	0.309	228841	0.273	0.036
East	7	0.395	248997	0.380	0.015
Southeast	21	0.654	220995	0.475	0.180
South	9	0.765	318571	0.611	0.154
Southwest	8	0.864	313631	0.746	0.118
West	7	0.951	329818	0.888	0.063
Northwest	4	1.000	261172	1.000	0.000

Dmax = 0.180 – therefore reject the H_0 and state that there is a significant difference in site location. In other words, sites are distributed non-randomly in relation to the aspect.

3.2 Distance to Lakes Statistical Testing

H_0 – There is no difference between the distribution of sites in relation distance to lakes and the general distribution of cells in the environment and their distance to lakes.
H_a – There is a difference between the distribution of sites in relation to distance to lakes and the general distribution of cells in the environment and their distance to lakes

Table 39: Distance to Lakes Statistical Testing

Distance to Lakes Buffer Distance	Sites	Cumulative Percent	Cells in the Environment	Cumulative Percent	Difference
100	73	0.901	181539	0.072	0.830
200	1	0.914	180623	0.143	0.771
300	0	0.914	181596	0.215	0.699
400	0	0.914	176552	0.285	0.629
500	1	0.926	166677	0.350	0.576
500+	6	1.000	1644659	1.000	0.000

Dmax = 0.830 – therefore reject the H_0 and state that there is a significant difference in site location. In other words, sites are distributed non-randomly in relation to the distance to lakes.

3.3 Distance to Rivers Statistical Testing

H_0 – There is no difference between the distribution of sites in relation distance to rivers and the general distribution of cells in the environment and their distance to rivers.
H_a – There is a difference between the distribution of sites in relation to distance to rivers and the general distribution of cells in the environment and their distance to rivers

Table 40: Distance to Rivers Statistical Testing

Distance to Rivers Buffer Distance	Sites	Cumulative Percent	Cells in the Environment	Cumulative Percent	Difference
100	0	0.000	152546	0.061	-0.061
200	0	0.000	156014	0.122	-0.122
300	1	0.012	156161	0.184	-0.172
400	0	0.012	154042	0.245	-0.233
500	3	0.049	149626	0.305	-0.255
500+	77	1.000	1752447	1.000	0.000

Dmax = 0.255 – therefore reject the H_0 and state that there is a significant difference in site location. In other words, sites are distributed non-randomly in relation to the distance to rivers.

3.4 Forest Resource Inventory Statistical Testing

H_0 – There is no difference between the distribution of sites in relation the forest resource inventory and the general distribution of cells in the environment and their forest resource inventory.
H_a – There is a difference between the distribution of sites in relation the forest resource inventory and the general distribution of cells in the environment and their forest resource inventory

Table 41: Forest Resource Inventory Statistical Testing

Tree Type	Sites	Cumulative Percent	Cells in the Environment	Cumulative Percent	Difference
Balsam Fir	15	0.1852	16679	0.0069	0.1782
Black Spruce	7	0.2716	200360	0.0904	0.1812
Hardwood	20	0.5185	654976	0.3632	0.1554
Jack Pine	26	0.8395	1152211	0.8430	-0.0035
Tamarack	0	0.8395	76471	0.8748	-0.0353
Trembling Aspen	13	1.0000	278419	0.9908	0.0092
White Spruce	0	1.0000	21190	0.9996	0.0004
Balsam Poplar	0	1.0000	259	0.9997	0.0003
Birch	0	1.0000	113	0.9998	0.0002
Ash	0	1.0000	287	0.9999	0.0001
Manitoba Maple	0	1.0000	277	1.0000	0.0000

Dmax = 0.1812 – therefore reject the H_0 and state that there is a significant difference in site location. In other words, sites are distributed non-randomly in relation to the forest resource inventory.

3.5 Slope Statistical Testing

H_0 – There is no difference between the distribution of sites in relation slope and the general distribution of cells in the environment and their slope.
H_a – There is a difference between the distribution of sites in relation the slope and the general distribution of cells in the environment and their Slope

Table 42: Slope Statistical Testing

Slope Class	Sites	Cumulative Percent	Cells in the Environment	Cumulative Percent	Difference
Flat	11	0.136	111100	0.048	0.088
0-5	45	0.691	2007558	0.910	-0.219
5-10	14	0.864	164661	0.981	-0.116
10-15	8	0.963	33955	0.995	-0.032
15+	3	1.000	11126	1.000	0.000

Dmax = 0.219 – therefore reject the H_0 and state that there is a significant difference in site location. In other words, sites are distributed non-randomly in relation to the slope.

Appendix 3: Environmental Variable Weightings

Table 43: Aspect Class Weighting

Category weighting = 4	
Flat	4
North	3
Northeast	3
East	2
Southeast	5
South	4
Southwest	6
West	2
Northwest	1

Table 44: Distance to Lakes Class Weighting

Category weighting = 6	
< 100 m	5
< 200 m	4
< 300 m	3
< 400 m	2
< 500 m	1
500 +m	0

Table 45: Distance to Rivers Class Weighting

Category weighting = 3	
< 100 m	5
< 200 m	4
< 300 m	3
< 400 m	2
< 500 m	1
500 +m	0

Table 46: Forest Resource Inventory Weighting

Category weighting = 4	
Balsam Fir	2
Black Spruce	1
Hardwood	3
Jack Pine	4
Tamarack	1
Trembling Aspen	3
White Spruce	0
Balsam Poplar	0
Birch	0
Ash	0
Manitoba Maple	0

Table 47: Slope Class Weighting

Category weighting = 4	
Flat	3
0-5 degrees slope	5
5-10 degrees slope	4
10-15 degrees slope	3
More than 15 degrees of slope	2

www.ingramcontent.com/pod-product-compliance
Lightning Source LLC
Chambersburg PA
CBHW061546010526
44113CB00023B/2816